lacy knits

lacy knits

20 Delicate Projects in Soft, Luxurious Mohair-Silk Yarns

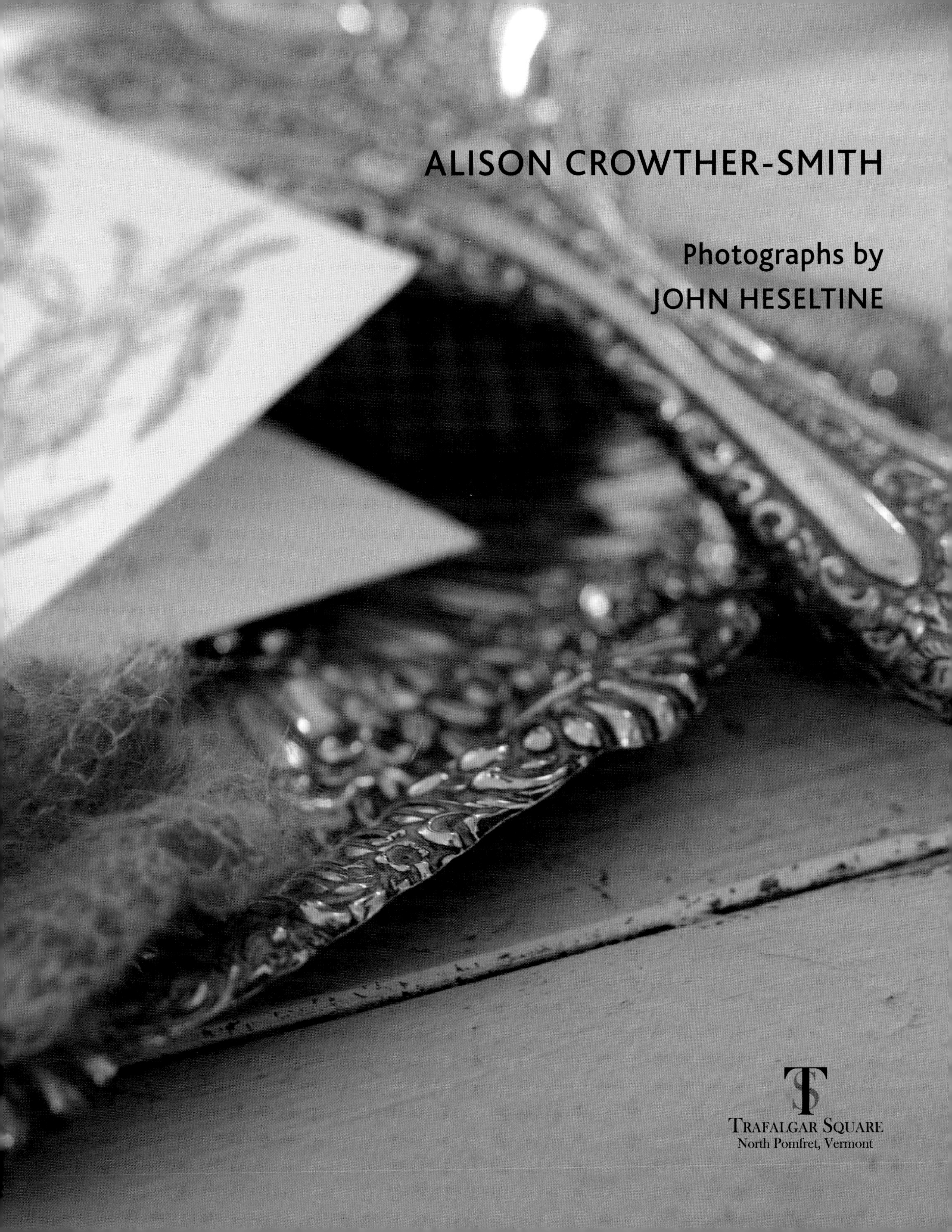

ALISON CROWTHER-SMITH

Photographs by
JOHN HESELTINE

TS

TRAFALGAR SQUARE
North Pomfret, Vermont

This book is dedicated to Hilda Farley and Jean Marshall. You know why. Thank you both so much.

First published in the United States of America in 2011 by Trafalgar Square Books
North Pomfret, Vermont 05053

Copyright © Berry & Bridges Ltd 2011
Project design copyright © Alison Crowther-Smith 2011

Created and produced by Berry & Bridges Ltd
Suite 416, Belsize Business Centre
258 Belsize Road
London NW6 4BT

Editor Katie Hardwicke
Designer Anne Wilson
Stylist Susan Berry
Pattern writer Penny Hill
Pattern checker Donna Jones

Publisher Susan Berry

A catalog record of this book is available from the Library of Congress

ISBN: 978-1-57076-463-9
Library of Congress Number: 2001012345

Reproduced and printed in Singapore

Contents

introduction

My love affair with fine mohair-silk yarn shows no signs of waning. Its appeal never dulls for me. It just grows.

When I designed the projects for *Silky Little Knits* a couple of years ago, I had a few basic principles to start with: to keep it fairly simple, in order to introduce knitters to the beauty of knitting with mohair-silk yarn; to explore ways of showing this super-fine yarn off to its best advantage, in terms of textures, embellishments, and with shade work; and to offer accessible, fairly quick-to-knit projects to busy knitters—like you and me. These principles still apply here—plus lace.

The most often used application for a yarn like Rowan's Kidsilk Haze, which I have used a lot in this book, is lace knitting. In this new book, each project features a lace element or it is all lace. Lace and Kidsilk Haze go together beautifully, with the yarn's already ethereal quality making lace stitches even more delicate.

However, some people are nervous about knitting lace patterns. So in *Lacy Knits*, my objectives were clear from the start: to offer a gentle, staged journey through lace knitting, whether you are new to lace or more experienced; to keep it as simple as possible, with the exception of one or two of the designs that are quite advanced lace knitting; and to give you some "traditional" items but with the balance towards modern applications for lace.

Knitting is something I do in order to relax, create, and unwind. Now I like a challenge as much as the next knitter, but if the "challenge" is too complicated the knitter will be turned off from the start. Lace can be tough. Just opening an advanced lace knitting book and seeing the charts, which look rather like a migraine expressed on paper, brings me out in a panic. There is none of that in this book.

In *Lacy Knits*, you will find some very easy lace patterns, some that have a higher element of challenge, and some that are more advanced. None is really difficult, in my view, but I have rated each project really honestly. You could, for example, start with the ones that have an easy rating, find out that you are unexpectedly good at them, and proceed to race through the intermediate category, and onto the advanced ones. I also offer you some modern interpretations of lace knitting, such as the Glow scarf on page 18, where I have combined mohair yarns of different weights and an unusual (but easy) lace stitch to make a scarf that stands out from more traditional items, or the Shimmer stole on page

42, where the lace content is an overlaid filigree effect in a contrasting yarn on top of the fine mohair—really easy, but very effective. I like traditional lace but I also like playing with ply, gauge, and textures to achieve unusual results.

I have a great fondness for knitting that makes it look as if you have worked really hard in order to achieve the results, whereas in fact you have only experienced a gentle challenge—enough to whet your interest, but not so much that you can only knit the pattern if you are left alone to do so. Silence is a scarce commodity in my household, so I generally can't be bothered with that level of difficulty. There are plenty of very gratifying projects in here, easier than they perhaps look to the people you choose to give them to. How satisfying is that?

Another thing. I like projects that I have a very good chance of finishing. I know my limits and a long and intricate pattern that will take me many weeks to work through is not my idea of fun. So, again, though some of the designs take a little longer, many could easily be knitted in a weekend or two and the emphasis is really on accessories—almost instant gratification.

On the following pages I have given you some tips and pointers for successful lace knitting. But what I want you to bear in mind, if lace is a new departure for you or if you have struggled in the past, is this: if you can knit and purl, you can knit lace.

I really do hope you enjoy the projects in this book and the approach I have taken to setting them out for you. I feel as if I have written it personally for each of you, just as it we were sitting and working on our lace knitting together. I hope you feel the same.

Alison

all about lace

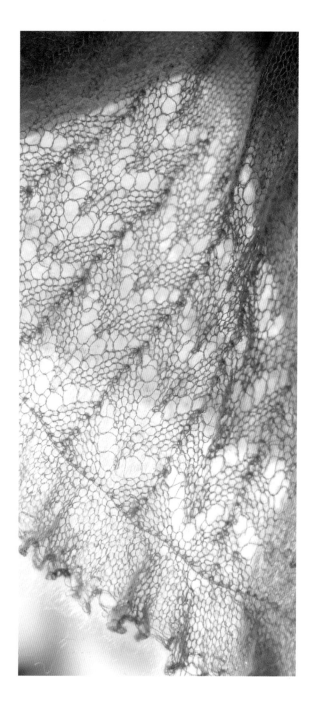

Lace knitting patterns may look intimidating but when you knit lace you are simply making knitted holes on purpose. We can all make holes by dropping stitches, but the key, obviously, is getting the holes where you want them and making sure they do not run!

Lace is actually logical: it's a sequence of stitches and rows, based on repeating these sequences. The longer the repeats, usually, and the fewer "resting"—or non-lace—rows you have, the harder lace is to work. But if you can knit and purl and increase and decrease, you *can* knit lace because that is all you are ever going to do.

You make the holes of lace by working decreasing stitches and balancing those with a corresponding increase. This is often in the same row and usually in the same repeat. Sometimes, the stitch count will vary between rows and, if so, the pattern will usually advise you not to count your stitches after these rows. The number will usually be made up later on in the row repeat or the following row.

Increasing and decreasing is done in various ways in lace knitting, depending on how you want the holes to look and how you want the stitches to slope.

INCREASES

An increase is usually worked by moving the yarn forward, or back, or actually around the needle. The movements to make an increase are very similar and even sound similar in the patterns. An increase is always worked by taking the yarn around the needle but in various ways, depending on the stitches you are working in the pattern (see "Lace knitting techniques," on page 10).

DECREASES

These are just the standard decreases you meet in any knitting pattern. The term K2tog (knit 2 stitches together), decreases your stitch count by 1 stitch. The term Sl 1, K1, psso or skpo (slip 1 stitch from the left-hand needle to the right without knitting it, knit 1 stitch, pass the slipped stitch over the knitted stitch), also decreases your stitch count by 1, but the work slopes the other way, so it balances the look of the K2tog instruction, as in my camisole pattern below, where we have a chevron-style lace pattern.

LACE TIPS

● Always practice a new lace pattern in an easy-to-knit yarn, such as a smooth wool or cotton. Once you have mastered the pattern, it will be much easier to knit your

project in the specified yarn, especially if it's a mohair blend, and it may also save you wasting some of your precious project yarn.

● Lace inevitably has repeats in it. The repeats will be both by stitches and also by rows. Just like gauge squares, really. Over a whole row the pattern will be broken down into these repeats, so if the pattern has a 6-stitch repeat, for example, that row will have a number of stitches divisible by 6. Often, the pattern will have a repeat PLUS some extra stitches to make it correct at the ends of rows. For example, a repeat of 6 stitches, plus 2 would mean that the pattern would have a number of stitches divisible by 6 plus the 2 extra stitches. Not all patterns say what the stitch repeat is, which I think is rather unhelpful, because you do really need to know this. So I always say what it is.

● I think you need to know this number because you may want to make the item wider or smaller, and you can really only do this by adding or removing repeats. Plus, I like to know what I'm doing and why. It makes the lace easier to tackle. Row repeats will be given in all patterns. This is the number of rows it will take you to complete one whole section of the lace pattern. Personally, if this looks to me more like a weekly shopping list than a knitting pattern, I tend to move on.

NOTE FOR ALL KNITTERS

To help novice knitters, I have broken down the more general yarn over and yarn forward abbreviations into more precisely worded ones (see pages 12–13 for visual reference) to describe how you move the yarn when knitting particular types of stitches, and have used these abbreviations in the patterns. If you prefer to translate these as the more general yo/yfwd instructions, then of course you are free to do so.

Opposite: The Luster cape (see page 72) showing increases.
Left: The Avalon camisole (see page 102) showing chevron-style decreases.

Lace knitting techniques

The techniques for lace knitting are not really different from any general techniques for increasing and decreasing, but because you make stitches in different ways, depending on whether you are working on a knit row, a purl row, or changing between knit and purl stitches and purl and knit stitches, we show here how this is done and also give in the patterns a special definition for each. The term often used for making an extra stitch or loop when you wrap the yarn around the needle to create a hole is a "yarn over." Although some patterns use this term (and its special abbreviation, yo), we have broken this down into separate abbreviations, depending on what is required in the pattern and show here how to work these particular yarn overs.

There is also another abbreviation we use which is too simple to warrant illustrated steps. When you need to move the yarn from the front to the back of the work, and from the back to the front of the work, without making a stitch—for example, when about to slip a stitch knitwise or purlwise, we give the instruction yarn to front (abbreviated as wyif) or yarn to back (wyib).

For a full list of the abbreviations used in this book see page 116.

Between the knit stitches (yfwd) to make a stitch
1 Bring the yarn from the back of the knitting to the front.

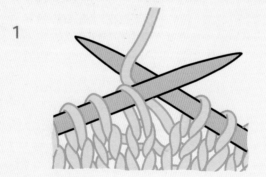

2 Now insert the right-hand needle tip into the next stitch, wrapping the yarn around the tip of the right needle to create a hole and make a new stitch.

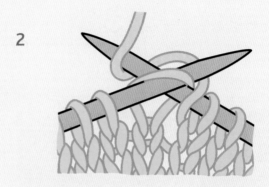

Between purl stitches (yrn) to make a stitch
1 Take the yarn over the right-hand needle to the back of the work (counterclockwise) and then bring it out between the points of the left- and right-hand needles to the front.

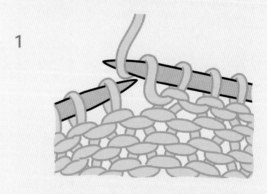

2 Purl the next stitch to create a hole and make a new stitch.

2

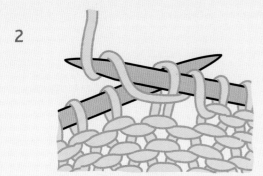

Between knit and purl stitches (yfrn)

1 After knitting a stitch, bring the yarn to the front, between the needles, as if to purl and then take the yarn over the tip of the right needle to the back of the work.

1

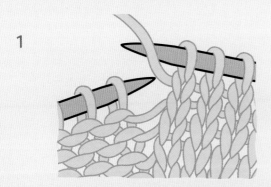

2 Bring the yarn forward again between the left- and right-hand needles to the front of the work. Purl the next stitch to create a hole and make a new stitch.

2

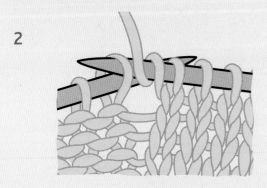

Between purl and knit stitches (yo)

1 After purling a stitch, with the yarn at the front, insert the needle into the next stitch knitwise and bring the yarn behind the left needle.

1

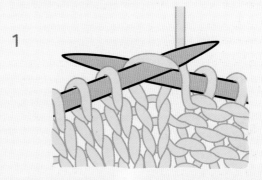

2 Wrap the yarn around the right-hand needle to create a hole and knit the new stitch to create a hole and make a new stitch.

2

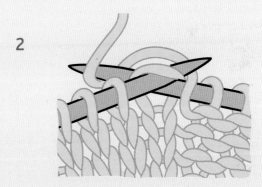

Suggestion After purling a stitch, with the yarn at the front, insert the needle into the next stitch knitwise. Continue to knit this stitch, taking the yarn over the right-hand needle as you do, thus creating a hole and a new stitch.

Other useful techniques

Thumb cast-on method

The thumb cast-on, also called the single or long-tail cast-on, is the easiest cast-on of all. Many of my patterns call for this cast-on or the cable cast-on (see opposite), as each creates a neat and even edge along the lower edge of the knitting. When my instructions say you can use either the thumb or cable cast-on, the choice is really up to you—use the one that you are the most comfortable with. Make sure you leave enough yarn to cast on all the stitches required in the pattern.

1 Make a slip knot as for any cast-on and place it on the right needle. Wrap the yarn coming from the ball around the back of your left thumb and hold it in the palm of your left hand as shown.

2 Insert the right needle from underneath into the loop around your left thumb.

3 Release the loop of yarn from your left thumb and gently pull the yarn to form the new loop on the right needle.

4 Wrap the yarn around your left thumb again and repeat steps 2 and 3 to make as many cast-on stitches as you need.

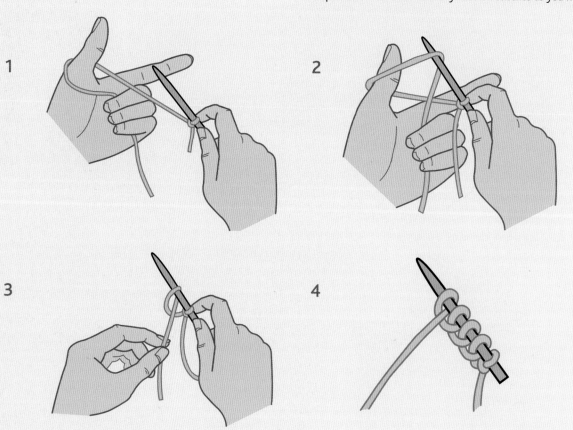

Cable cast-on method

The cable cast-on method gives you a firm edge with a line along the lower edge of the knitting. I often use this cast-on or the thumb cast-on (see opposite) when a neat, even, distinct edge is appropriate.

1 Make a slip knot as for any cast-on and place it on the left needle. Then knit into the slip knot and slip the new stitch back onto the left needle as for steps 1 and 2 of the lace cast-on (see page 14). Next, insert the right needle between the two stitches on the left needle as shown and knit a stitch through this space.

2 Insert the left needle into the resulting new stitch as shown by the arrow (from right to left through the front of the stitch) and slip it onto the left needle.

3 There are now three stitches on the left needle.

4 To make the following cast-on stitches, insert the right needle between the first two stitches on the left needle and knit a stitch through this space. Again, transfer this stitch back onto the left needle. Repeat this step to make as many cast-on stitches as you need.

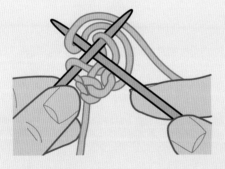

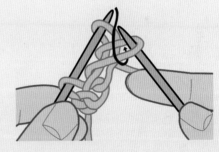

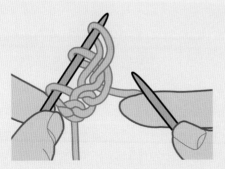

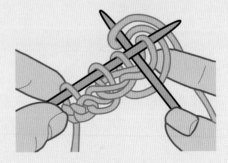

Lace cast-on method

Also called the knit cast-on, this is a cast-on that gives a lacy, open edge. Since as a rule it is best to have a nice firm lower edge on knitting, the lace cast-on is not used often. The more popular thumb and cable cast-on methods give you a firm edge with a line along the lower edge (see pages 12 and 13). However, for lace, the work should look as if the lace just started—no line along the lower edge. Throughout the patterns in this book, I usually specify which kind of cast-on is most suitable.

1 Make a slip knot as for any cast-on and place it on the left needle. Insert the right needle into the slip knot and knit the stitch in the usual way, but keep the slip knot on the left needle.

2 Insert the left needle into the resulting new stitch as shown by the arrow (from right to left through the front of the stitch) and slip it onto the left needle.

3 To make the next cast-on stitch, insert the right needle into the stitch just transferred back to the left needle, and knit a stitch in the usual way. Again, transfer this stitch back onto the left needle.

4 Repeat step 3 to make as many cast-on stitches as you need. If you want to tighten these cast-on loops, you can work into the back of each stitch on the first row—but for a lacy, open edge, work into the front of the cast-on stitches in the usual way.

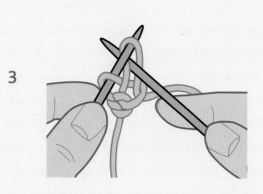

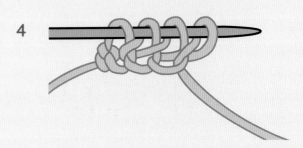

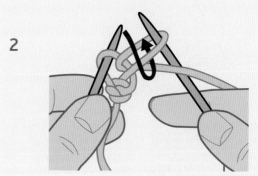

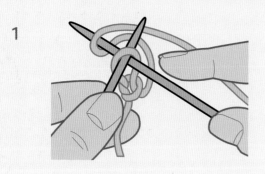

Knitting in the round with four needles

Follow these simple steps for knitting in the round with a set of four double-pointed needles. Double-pointed needles are usually sold in sets of five. You can use three plus a working needle for small items as shown here, or four plus your working needle when you have more stitches. The first two or three rounds will be the hardest, and after that it all falls into place. Remember that when you work stockinette stitch in the round, you only work in knit stitch as you only ever work on the right side, round and round.

1 Cast on all the stitches required onto one of the needles. Then distribute the stitches evenly onto three of the double-pointed needles, leaving the fourth needle to knit with. Take care when moving the stitches along not to twist the work.

2 Hold the three needles with the stitches on them in a ring as shown, again making sure the stitches are not twisted.

3 Place a stitch marker on the right needle at the end of the cast-on stitches—this is to mark the beginning/end of each row. (You can use a plastic stitch marker or simply make your own stitch marker by tying a little ring with a piece of contrasting cotton yarn.) Now insert the tip of the fourth needle into the first stitch on the left needle to join the work together and begin the first stitch of the first round. Continue to knit round and round, slipping the stitch marker each time you reach it.

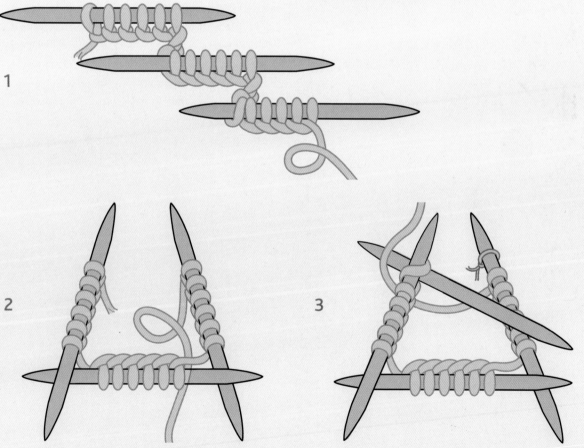

1

2

3

Knitting with beads and sequins

This is an invaluable technique and one that I am sure you will use to adorn all your luxury-mohair knitting. Beads and sequins are positioned in the same way, although sequins do not lie down as easily and neatly as the beads, unless you get sequins with holes at one side rather than in the middle. If you want clusters of beads, thread on more to start with and move and position two or three beads together.

If you are using a bead on top of a sequin, you carry it out exactly the same as for the single bead or sequin, just move them along together. However, if you want the bead on top of the sequin, which you will, you must thread them on in the right order. Remember that whatever you thread on LAST will be the FIRST item to come off the yarn. So you must start threading with a bead and end with a sequin: bead, sequin, bead, sequin, and so on.

1 Thread on the beads or sequins before you cast on with the yarn. To do this, thread a fine sewing needle with a short length of sewing thread. (Check first that the beads and sequins you have chosen will fit over this needle.) Tie the two ends of the thread together to form a loop and hang the tail-end of your yarn through the loop. With the tip of this needle, pick up the bead or sequin and pass this along the needle, down the thread, and thus onto the yarn; you can pick up several beads or sequins together. (If you need to use hundreds of beads on a single ball of yarn, you can add them gradually, breaking the yarn each time you need to add more.)

2 When you want to place a bead or sequin, which will appear in the pattern as "*bead 1*" or "*place sequin and bead*," bring the yarn to the front (the right side) of the work between the two needles. Then slide a bead or sequin (or a sequin and bead together) up close to the stitch just worked. Slip the next stitch purlwise from the left-hand needle to the right-hand needle, inserting the right-hand needle from right to left through the front of the stitch. Then take the yarn back to the wrong side of the work as shown here, leaving the bead or sequin sitting on the right side of the work on top of the slipped stitch. The pattern will now state what you need to do next, usually knit the next stitch.

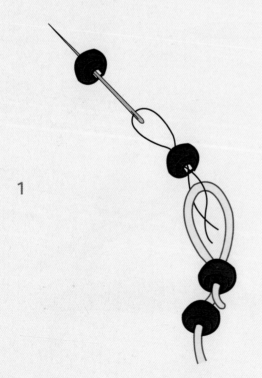

1

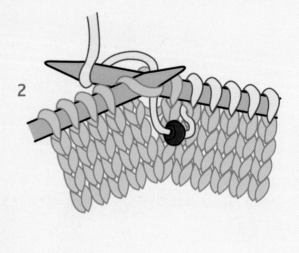

2

Picking up stitches for frills

To make the many frills that feature in the book, I have used the technique of picking up stitches—a method you will already be familiar with if you have ever added a button band or collar to a knitted garment piece. You may also need to pick up stitches along the cast-on edge or the side edge of the knitting, and the method for doing this is the same.

1 Hold the knitting with the right or wrong side facing as instructed. Then working from right to left along the edge of the knitting, insert the tip of the needle through the first bound-off loop. (The needle is shown here inserted under both loops of the bound-off stitch, but for the double frills along a bound-off edge you will be asked to pick up loops through one loop only of the bound-off stitch.)

2 Wrap the yarn being used for the frill around the tip of the needle as shown and pull it through with the tip of the needle, just as if you are knitting a stitch through the bound-off loop.

3 This forms a loop on the needle. Insert the needle through the top of the next bound-off loop and pull the yarn through the next stitch in the same way.

4 Continue along the edge in this way, ensuring that you are picking up the stitches evenly along the edge.

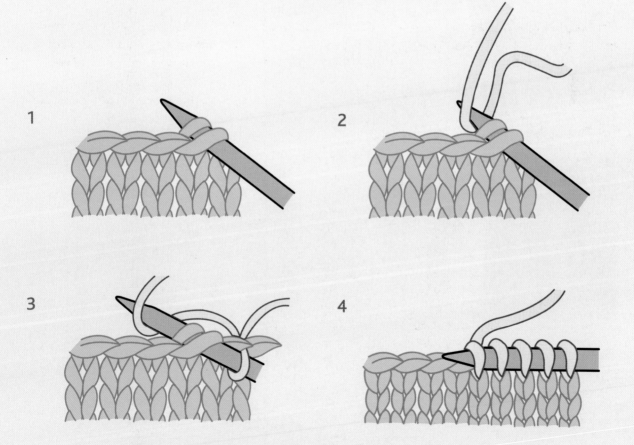

1

2

3

4

glow scarf

This scarf is truly versatile. During the dark winter months, having some lovely yarns to knit a cozy scarf with will brighten up your evenings. The colors of this scarf are, to me, perfect, because they go so well together and make each other (and the wearer) positively *glow*. Then, in summer, it turns into the perfect accessory to drape over a sleeveless top!

This design is based on the much under-rated yet often knitted garter stitch, but with a very modern lace twist. It is knitted on big fat needles and it really races along, because on six of the eight rows in the repeat, you are just knitting. However, boredom does not set in because you are busy changing yarns every two rows and for two rows there is some easy but satisfying activity to vary the pace.

Kidsilk Aura and *Kidsilk Haze* are sister yarns—the DNA of the yarns is the same but in all other respects they differ, although they do get along together. Knitted in stripes, the über-fluffy *Aura* seeks to dominate the slight *Kidsilk Haze* but the big personality of the *Kidsilk Haze* is more than a match. This scarf uses the varying plys to add further texture to the lacy pattern. I allow the *Kidsilk Haze* to do the lace rows because it makes them stand out even more. So, you get the light-shining-from-a-winter-window effect of the round lace stitches balanced by the fatness of the *Aura's* garter stitch frame. It's modern lace and it makes the most of these lovely yarns.

It also undulates, at the sides. I like this effect and it's a feature of the ply-mixing, but I added the garter stitch border at each end to even this out a little. However, these yarns do have curves, and I like to let them show.

Both the yarns I have used have a wide palette, so if you like a warmer palette, there are colorways for you.

SKILL LEVEL
Easy

SIZE OF SCARF
The finished scarf measures approximately 58¼in/148cm long by 11½in/29cm wide.

YOU WILL NEED
Yarn A   1 x ⁷⁄₈oz/25g ball of Rowan *Kidsilk Haze* in lime green (Jelly, 597)

Yarn B   2 x ⁷⁄₈oz/25g balls of Rowan *Kidsilk Aura* in teal (Mallard, 769)

Pair of size 10 (6mm) needles

GAUGE
18 sts and 15 rows knitted to 4in/10cm square measured over lace pattern using both yarns and size 10 (6mm) needles *or needle size necessary to obtain correct gauge.*

SPECIAL ABBREVIATIONS
cluster 5 With the tip of the RH needle, slip the next 5 sts, purlwise, onto the RH needle, dropping the extra loops made on the previous row as you do so. Slip these 5 long sts back onto the LH needle. Then, *working them all together as one stitch—all five loops are worked together—*K, P, K, P, and K again into the st.

Note You are NOT knitting into the front and back of the st as in a conventional increase, say for a bobble, you are working actual K and P actions, but not finishing the stitch and slipping it off until the last one is complete. Note also that you will be knitting into the front of the st on the K move, in the normal way *and* you will be moving your working yarn backward and forward, to be in the correct position to either knit or purl.

See also page 116.

PATTERN NOTE
Yarns are held SINGLE throughout.

ALISON'S TIPS
● Practice the cluster 5 st by knitting a small test piece (twice the 8-row repeat) in a smooth wool yarn. It's a multiple of 5 (plus 3 sts at each end to give a little border), so just play about with 26 sts and follow the actual pattern below.

● Carry the non-working yarns up the side to save hours of sewing in.

● Give each side a fair bit of play with the yarns—don't pull or tighten up here or the edges of the knitting will become too wavy.

TO MAKE SCARF
Using size 10 (6mm) needles and yarn A, cast on 51 sts using the thumb method (see page 12), loosely.

Row 1 Using yarn A, knit.

Row 2 Knit.

Change to yarn B.

Row 3 Knit.

Row 4 Knit.

Change to yarn A.

Row 5 K3, *K1, winding the yarn round the needle 3 times, rep from * to last 3 sts, K3.

Row 6 K3, *cluster 5, rep from * to last 3 sts, K3.

Change to yarn B.

Row 7 Knit.

Row 8 Knit.

These 8 rows form patt.

Cont in patt until scarf measures approx. 57¾in/147cm, ending with Row 8.

Change to yarn A.

Work 2 rows in garter st and then bind off loosely to match cast-on end.

Sew in ends.

Referring to ball bands for instructions, with WS facing, pin out and lightly press with a cool iron and slightly damp cloth, not pressing down with the iron. Let dry fully before unpinning.

Go forth and glow!

sunday night mittens

Sunday nights, especially in the fall and winter, are a great time to snuggle down on the sofa with a good book or to watch a movie. Being someone who "feels the cold," when I look at some of the flimsy period costumes, I tend to think the heroines would feel better if their hands were warm, at least.

For those of you who want to wear something elegant but don't want cold hands, I offer you these Sunday Night fingerless mittens. Being in this book, they must be lacy. So, knitted on my sofa, but with a period heroine in mind, here they are! They are in Rowan *Pure Wool 4 Ply*, which is a very soft and polite yarn, knitted together with *Kidsilk Haze*. I have knitted them on small needles, and start and finish with a conventional K3, P3 rib, with an easy-going lace rib design for the main part of the mitten. The mittens are thumbless, so there are no gusset issues to deal with. You make the thumb-hole by the simple but ingenious device of not knitting in the round for a while, and then resuming again. The *Kidsilk Haze* lends glamour and extra warmth to the design and as both yarns are ultra-soft, they feel very luxurious.

The yarn mixing gives you a gorgeous tweedy effect without any of the tweedy scratch and you can be subtle with the toning shades or go wild and clash your colors—both yarns have a huge palette. They are finished with a tiny frill just using the *Kidsilk Haze*. They are super-quick to knit—you will easily finish a pair in a few evenings.

SKILL LEVEL
Intermediate

SIZE OF MITTENS
The finished mittens measure approximately 8½in/21cm long, including frill, and 6¾in/17cm in circumference at widest (lacy) point.

YOU WILL NEED
Yarn A 1 x ⁷/₈oz/25g ball of Rowan *Kidsilk Haze* in mallard blue (Trance, 582)

Yarn B 1 x 1¾oz/50g ball of Rowan *Pure Wool 4 Ply* in light green (Sage, 448)

Pair of size 3 (3mm) needles

1 set of size 3 (3mm) double-pointed needles

Stitch marker

GAUGE
28 sts and 36 rows to 4in/10cm square measured over rib pattern, when slightly stretched widthways, using yarns A and B held together and size 3 (3mm) needles *or needle size necessary to obtain correct gauge.*

ABBREVIATIONS
See page 116.

ALISON'S TIPS
• The rib is a K3, P3 rib at the start and the finish, and the lace is a 6-st repeat, so it is a great help to have the stitches arranged in a number divisible by 6 on each needle.

• If you don't want the frill, bind off in rib; if you do want the frill, bind off knitwise.

• If you need to do a yo at the start of an empty double-pointed needle, just get it into position to purl, and then wrap the yarn round it and back to the front again to work—the loop you made is just the same as if it was in the middle of a needle and works fine.

• My hands are small but not especially slender. If you want a tight fit, take off 6 sts. For a child, take off approximately 12 and reduce the length.

• I stayed on my double-pointed needles for the flat knitting bit because it's not for long but you could go onto conventional single-pointed needles here if you want.

TO MAKE MITTENS (make 2)
Using size 3 (3mm) needles and yarns A and B held together cast on 48 sts using the thumb method (see page 12).

Place marker to mark beg and end of the round.

Next round *K3, P3, rep from * to end of round.

Cont in rib for 1¼in/3cm (or more if you want a longer cuff).

Round 1 *Yrn, P3tog, yrn, P1, K1, P1; rep from * to end of round.

Round 2 *K3, P1, K1, P1; rep from * to end of round.

Round 3 As Round 2.

Round 4 As Round 2.

These 4 rounds complete the lace rib patt.

Continue in the lace rib until the mitt measures the required length to the base of your thumb but making sure you finish after Round 3.

Next round Slip the marker off.

Turn and work in ROWS, in lace rib (remember you're working Row 4 first).

Row 1 *Yrn, P3tog, yrn, P1, K1, P1, rep from * to end of row, turn.

Rows 2 and 4 (WS) *K1, P1, K1, P3, rep from * to end of row, turn.

Row 3 *K3, P1, K1, P1, rep from * to end of row, turn.

Starting with Row 4, work 18 rows in pattern, then check length by slipping your hand in. Add an even number of rows if necessary.

Join up again to knit in the round after working a Row 1 or Row 3, placing marker. Cont in the lace patt in the round until the mitten is as long up your hand as required less 1¼in/3cm for frill.

Change to K3, P3 rib (as at the cuff) for ⁵/₈in/1.5cm.

Bind off.

FRILL

Using size 3 (3mm) double-pointed needles and yarn A held single, with RS facing, pick up (see page 17) and knit 48 sts around the finger opening of the mitt. (I picked these up over 3 needles.) Place marker and join to knit in the round.

Next round *K into the front and back of the next st, rep from * to end. *96 sts*.

Next round As last round. *192 sts*.

Bind off loosely.

Sew in ends. Do not press.

I think this is a perfect scarf for a lace-beginner, the pattern is very easy and quick to master, as it only has a two-row repeat, and one of these is just purling straight across the row. But mainly, once you have done two or three repeats, it's glaringly obvious where you have gone wrong (if you should go wrong, which I confidently predict you will not), and it's simple to fix because there is only the one lace-action row to deal with.

The simplest design ideas often make an item a bit special. In this case it's a combination of the puffed cast-on edge (achieved by the clever method of reverse stockinette stitch rows to start with) plus the berry shades used for the colorwash. The ends look as if they have been dipped in blackberry juice and the color has faded as it "bleeds" up the scarf. However, I am certain that if your color choices are, say, greens, aquas, or warm autumnal shades, it will work just as well. For a similar effect in terms of subtle color changes, choose three toning shades and start with the darkest at the bottom. The shade range is huge in *Kidsilk Haze*.

Because I have used the yarn held double, it creates a scarf that is very warm and comforting but still light. You have to use two strands to achieve the colorwash effect. But if you wanted stripes rather than this faded color transition, or a plain scarf, and you wanted it to be more floaty, it will also look lovely if knitted with one strand of yarn only—and, of course, you will need less yarn.

SKILL LEVEL
Easy

SIZE OF SCARF
The finished scarf measures approximately 61½in/156cm long by 9in/24cm wide.

YOU WILL NEED
Yarn A   1 x ⁷/₈oz/25g ball of Rowan's *Kidsilk Haze* in purple (Blackcurrant, 641)

Yarn B   1 x ⁷/₈oz/25g ball of Rowan's *Kidsilk Haze* in deep red (Liqueur, 595)

Yarn C   2 x ⁷/₈oz/25g balls of Rowan's *Kidsilk Haze* in mid-pink (Blushes, 583)

2 pairs of size 6 (4mm) needles
Stitch holder

GAUGE
27 sts and 23 rows to 4in/10cm square measured over lace pattern using yarn held double and size 6 (4mm) needles *or needle size necessary to obtain correct gauge.*

ABBREVIATIONS
See page 116.

PATTERN NOTES
This pattern is a multiple of 11 sts, so make it as wide as you wish, but don't forget you will need more yarn if you are making it wider than the one here.
Yarn is held DOUBLE throughout.
The scarf is made in two halves which are bound off together but if you prefer you can graft or Kitchener st them together.

TO MAKE SCARF (make two pieces alike)
Using size 6 (4mm) needles and two strands of yarn A held together, cast on 66 sts using the thumb method (see page 12) or use the cable method (see page 13) with a larger needle size.
Row 1 (RS) Purl.

Row 2 (WS) Knit.
Rep last 2 rows twice more.
Row 7 (RS) *K2tog, K3, yfwd, K1, yfwd, K3, K2tog, rep from * to end.
Row 8 Purl.
Rows 7 and 8 form the patt.
Cont in patt until scarf measures 3½in/9cm.
Cut off 1 strand of yarn A and join in 1 strand of yarn B.
Cont in patt until scarf measures 7¹/₈in/18cm.
Cut off rem strand of yarn A and join in second strand of yarn B.
Cont in patt until scarf measures 11in/28cm.
Cut off 1 strand of yarn B and join in 1 strand of yarn C.
Cont in patt until scarf measures 15in/39cm.
Cut off rem strand of yarn B and join in second strand of yarn C.
Cont in patt until scarf measures 30¾in/78cm, ending with Row 7 on one piece and Row 8 on other piece.
Note Finished scarf will be double this length so make any adjustment to length here if you want a longer scarf.
Do not bind off. Leave sts on a spare needle or st holder.

TO FINISH
With right sides together and both needles pointing in the same direction, bind off both pieces together using a third needle. Using yarn C held double, knit the first st from both needles together, then knit the next st from both needles together, pass first st over second st (binding it off) to end of row. Fasten off.
Sew in ends.
Referring to ball bands for instructions, with WS facing, pin out and very lightly press scarf, use a cool iron and a cloth, taking care not to press down at all. Do not press reverse stockinette st borders. Let dry fully before unpinning.

peony corsage

A small but perfectly formed homage to one of my favorite flowers, the peony. The best real-life peonies are, in my opinion, the ones that have a bowl-like base layer with masses of frothy petals crammed into the center. So in this corsage, you knit a lacy-edged base layer that is lightly bowl-shaped and then knit the center petals with the little flowers that I have also used on the camisole top (see page 102) and the cream stole (see page 68). But note that different needle sizes are used in each pattern. I knitted the stole and this corsage in the same yarns so they will go together and, if you do the same, you can use the leftover yarns from the stole.

The base layer is a multiple of 5 stitches plus 2, so you can make the peonies larger or smaller as preferred. I knitted the base with the yarn held double, except for the cast-on edge, because it needs a bit of body. The center blossoms are knitted with the yarn held single to keep it light. I put three in but by all means have more if you can cram them in!

On the outer edge, the lace section starts with dainty shell-like scallops and then there is a plain center section, where the gentle decreasing also happens. This causes the outer edge to fold gently inward, giving the bowl shape.

This corsage takes a tiny quantity of yarn, so it's an ideal "stash-buster." The edging in a contrasting shade, though, makes all the difference and takes only a few yards, so use up some of your leftovers. It takes about two hours to knit.

SKILL LEVEL
Easy

SIZE OF CORSAGE
The finished corsage measures approximately 4in/10cm in diameter.

YOU WILL NEED
Yarn A   Scrap of Rowan *Kidsilk Haze* in soft gray (Majestic, 589)

Yarn B   1 x 25g/⅞oz ball of Rowan *Kidsilk Haze* in cream (Cream, 634)

(If you have knitted the cream flower stole, you should have enough left to knit this, too.)

Pair of size 8 (5mm) needles

Pair of size 6 (4mm) needles

Pair of size 3 (3.25mm) needles

18 crystal beads (Size 6 seed beads)

Safety pin or brooch back

GAUGE
20 sts and 28 rows to 4in/10cm square measured over st st, using yarn held double and size 6 (4mm) needles. However, gauge is not critical with this item.

ABBREVIATIONS
See page 116.

TO MAKE CORSAGE
Outer flower (make 1)
Using size 8 (5mm) needles and yarn A, cast on 57 sts using the lace cast-on method (see page 14).

Change to yarn B held double and size 6 (4mm) needles.

Row 1 (RS) K1, yfwd, *K5, sl the 2nd, 3rd, 4th, and 5th of these 5 sts over the first st (the one closest to the tip of the RH needle), one at a time, yfwd, rep from * to last st, K1. *23 sts.*

Row 2 P1, *[P1, yo, K1tbl] all into the next st, P1, rep from *to end. *45 sts.*

Row 3 K2, K1tbl, *K3, K1tbl, rep from * to last 2 sts, K2.

Row 4 Knit.

Rows 5, 6, and 7 K1, *yfwd, K2tog, rep from * to end.

Row 8 Knit.

Row 9 (RS) Knit.

Row 10 Purl.

Row 11 *K3, K2tog, rep from * to end. *36 sts.*

Row 12 Purl.

Row 13 *K2, K2tog, rep from * to end. *27 sts.*

Row 14 Purl.

Row 15 *K1, K2tog, rep from * to end. *18 sts.*

Row 16 Purl.

Break yarn leaving approx. 8in/20cm tail. Do not bind off. Thread tail onto a yarn needle and thread the tail through the "live" sts, slipping them off the knitting needle as you go. Draw gently to close. Using this tail, and on WS, sew up the seam to form the bowl shape. Sew in ends. You do not need to press the flower, just lay it on a towel, flattened out, and put another towel with a book on top for about an hour so it lies flat but retains the cupped edges.

Center flowers (make 3)
Using size 3 (3.25mm) needles and yarn A held single, and lace cast-on method (see page 14), *cast on 4 sts, bind off 2 sts, slip st on RH needle onto the LH needle, rep from * until 34 sts are cast on.

Change to yarn B.

Row 1 (RS) Knit.

Row 2 Purl.

Row 3 Knit.

Row 4 *P2tog, rep from * to end. *17 sts.*

Row 5 K1, *K2tog, rep from * to end. *9 sts.*

Cut yarn leaving 6in/15cm tail. Thread tail onto a yarn needle and slip the 9 "live" sts off the knitting needle and onto and off the yarn needle; draw yarn to close the flower, spread it out and secure. Do not press. Leave tail to sew flower onto outer flower.

Sew flowers onto the center flower base, sewing 2 clusters of 3 beads into the center of each to finish.

netta lacy cuffs

How often one really wants one's wrist warming up with a *Kidsilk Haze* cuff is, perhaps, open to some debate. However, the fact that these are just very pretty, sweetly old-fashioned, and super-fast to knit more than closes that debate, I feel. Pop these on so they lie over the hand, peeping out from under your winter coat or sweater sleeve and I guarantee you will not be able to resist some serious hand-posing. They have the added bonus, worn under a smart winter coat sleeve, of making it look as if you're wearing an entire cream lace hand-knitted sweater, with only the lovely cuffs showing. I think they look equally good in casual mode, under your sweater sleeve, and teamed with jeans and boots, as they do dressed up with a black cashmere coat for a night out.

The lace element is the bit that lies over your hand and this is where the cuffs are cast on, weighted with a few beads. I knitted this part flat and then, for the ribbing section, I started knitting in the round. You don't have to, as you can continue flat and then seam the whole cuff, but I just like an unseamed rib; if you do knit the cuff flat, you need to add two extra stitches for seaming.

I also knitted the lace with the yarn held single for maximum airiness and the rib with yarn double for extra grip.

The ribbon is purely decorative, threaded through the eyelets and allowed to hang down. You really can't tie a wrist ribbon without help! A pair of these, including the beads, weighs only a few ounces, so they are a great way to use up leftovers of *Kidsilk Haze*.

SKILL LEVEL
Easy to intermediate

SIZE OF CUFFS
The finished cuff measures 6¼in/16cm from cast-on to bound-off edges; cuff measures 5½in/14cm in circumference at wrist.

YOU WILL NEED
1 x ⁷/₈oz/25g ball of Rowan *Kidsilk Haze* in cream (Cream, 634)
Pair of size 6 (4mm) needles
Pair of size 3 (3mm) needles (double-pointed if knitting the cuff in the round/single-pointed if knitting the cuff flat)
68 crystal beads (Size 6 seed beads)
1yd/1m ribbon, ⁵/₈in/1.5cm wide
Stitch marker

GAUGE
25 sts and 36 rows measured over 4in/10cm square in rib pattern, using yarn double and size 3 (3mm) needles *or needle size necessary to obtain correct gauge.*

SPECIAL ABBREVIATIONS
bead 2 Place 2 beads (see page 16).
See also page 116.

ALISON'S TIPS
• In this pattern you place the beads with the WS facing, though the beads still show on the RS. To place 2 beads from the WS, purl to the stitch where you want to place the beads, bring 2 beads up the yarn close to the needle, move yarn back (as if to knit), with beads on it, slip the next stitch from the left-hand needle to the right-hand needle; move yarn forward (as if to purl), leaving beads sitting on the slipped stitch—they will be at the back (RS) of the work; work next stitch as pattern indicates.

• If you don't want to add the ribbon, instead of working the eyelet row, knit to end.

TO MAKE CUFFS (make 2)
Thread 34 beads onto yarn held single (see page 16 for instruction on threading beads).
Using size 6 (4mm) needles cast on 71 sts using the lace cast-on method (see page 14).
Bead Row (WS) *P3, bead 2, rep from * to last 2 sts, P2.
Row 1 (RS) *K1, yfwd, K3, skpo, yfwd, sk2po, yfwd, K2tog, K3, yfwd, rep from * to last st, K1.
Row 2 Purl.
These two rows form lace pattern.
Repeat patt rows 5 times (making 12 patt rows worked in all, plus the bead row, giving 13 rows in total).
Work 2 rows in st st.
Change to size 3 (3mm) double-pointed needles and use yarn double. Place sts evenly over 3 needles and knit with 4th needle (or use a short circular needle if you prefer). Join to work in the round, placing marker to mark beg and end of rounds.
Next round K3, *K2tog, K4, rep from * to last 2 sts, K2. *60 sts.*
Next round Knit.
Next round *K3, K2tog, rep from * to end. *48 sts.*
Next round Knit.
Next round *K2, K2tog, rep from * to end. *36 sts.*
Next round Knit.
Knit for 10 rounds.
Next round (eyelet round) *K3, yfwd, K2tog, rep from * to last st, K1.
Knit for 2 rounds.
Next round *K2, P2, rep from * to end.
This round forms 2 x 2 rib. Work this round until rib measures approx. 2in/5cm.
Bind-off row *Cast on 2 sts, using lace cast-on method, bind off 4 sts, transfer the st on the RH needle to the LH needle, rep from * to end.
Fasten off. Sew in ends.
Turn cuff WS out and referring to ball band for care instructions, very lightly press the lace section only, using a damp pressing cloth and cool iron. Let dry. Sew up the lace

section. Cut the ribbon in half and thread through the eyelets, allowing it to hang down at the middle.

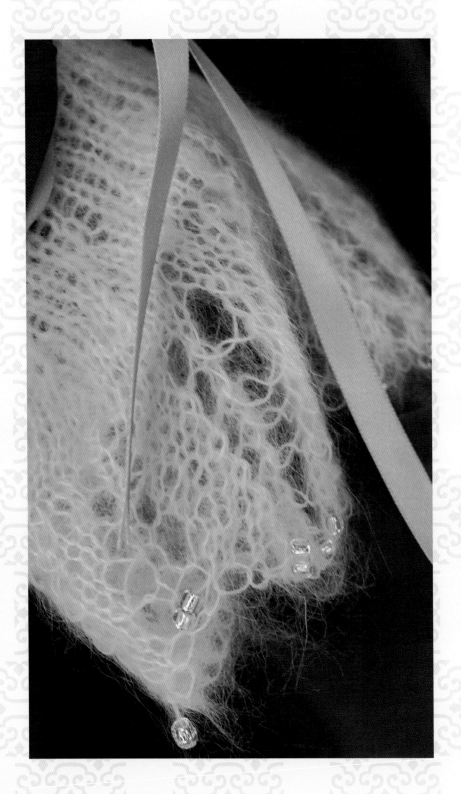

hush pillow

This pillow is rather luxurious and is based on the principle of letting the lace do all the showing off. First, buy a lovely but inexpensive pillow already covered in a plain but jewel-bright fabric cover—I chose vivid peacock blue in dull silk from a "value" store for a few dollars. Then choose your yarns to go with it. I wanted it to blend in with an element of contrast, so I chose a really pale soft blue-green for the *Milk Cotton* and a peacock or mallard blue shade for the *Kidsilk Haze*.

The finer *Milk Cotton*, which is a 4-ply yarn, and the *Kidsilk Haze* are knitted together, so they also blend and create a lovely fuzzy glow of mohair rising off the super-smooth cotton yarn. The color effect is very pleasing and as I gaze at the shade charts, I can see at least another six combinations that would also work well. You could go for toning as I did, or for contrasting.

The lace is open and has plenty of "holes" through which you see the lovely peacock blue silk. The only sewing involves stitching the pillow front to the back. Once the colored pillow is inserted, the lace stretches happily across it and your work is done.

Not a particularly hard lace pattern, this has a predictable rhythm, as the wrong side rows, though not just purl, are all the same and have an easy repeat. Also, the *Milk Cotton* makes the *Kidsilk Haze* behave itself due to its calming influence on the mohair!

SKILL LEVEL
Intermediate

SIZE OF PILLOW
The finished pillow cover measures 15in/38cm before sewing.

YOU WILL NEED
Yarn A   4 x 1¾oz/50g balls of Rowan *Fine Milk Cotton* in very pale blue-green (Apple Pips, 482)

Yarn B   2 x ⁷/₈oz/25g balls of Rowan *Kidsilk Haze* in mallard blue (Trance, 582)

Pair of size 8 (5mm) needles

1 pillow form (with matching plain bright cover), 15¾in/40cm square

GAUGE
16 sts and 23 rows to 4in/10cm square measured over lace patt using yarns A and B held together and size 8 (5mm) needles *or needle size necessary to obtain correct gauge.*

ABBREVIATIONS
See page 116.

ALISON'S TIPS
•   I only used a few ounces of the second ball of *Kidsilk Haze*; you may find one ball is enough, but best to say two just in case your gauge varies from mine.

•   You could knit the front and back in one piece by completing the front section, binding it off, and then with right side facing, pick up and knit 61 sts along cast-on edge. Then starting with Row 2, complete back as for the front, making one seam fewer to sew.

•   While it's not a difficult pattern, it is intermediate. I suggest you try a couple of repeats in just the *Fine Milk Cotton*, which you can pull back and re-use, to get the hang of it. The pattern is a multiple of 12 sts plus 1, so you could cast on 25 or 37 stitches to practice.

•   I think a lap-throw in this pattern would be lovely too, maybe using the *Fine Milk Cotton* plus the *Kidsilk Haze*, and increasing the size of your needles by a gauge or two to keep it nice and open.

TO MAKE PILLOW PANEL (make 2)
Using size 8 (5mm) needles and yarns A and B held together, cast on 61 sts using the thumb or cable method (see pages 12 and 13).

Lace pattern

Row 1 (RS) K1, *yfwd, K2tog, yfwd, skpo, K3, K2tog, yfwd, K3, rep from * to end.

Row 2 (WS) and all alternate rows P1, *yrn, P2tog, P10, rep from * to end.

Row 3 K1, *yfwd, K2tog, yfwd, K1, skpo, K1, K2tog, K1, yfwd, K3, rep from * to end.

Row 5 K1, *yfwd, K2tog, K1, K2tog, yfwd, K1, yfwd, skpo, K4, rep from * to end.

Row 7 K1, *yfwd, [K2tog] twice, K1, [yfwd, K1] twice, skpo, K3, rep from * to end.

Row 8 As Row 2.

These 8 rows form lace patt. Rep Rows 1 to 8 until work is 15in/38cm long (11 patt repeats).

TO FINISH
With WS facing, pin the two sides out to 15in/38cm square and, referring to ball bands for instructions, very lightly press using a slightly damp pressing cloth and no actual pressure. Remove cloth and Let dry fully before unpinning. With RS facing together, sew the pillow sides together on three sides. Turn RS facing out. Insert pillow form. Close fourth side using overcasting stitch.

shimmer stole

The more observant may have noticed that I am a big fan of glitter. Beads and sequins attract me in a way that I never try to resist. So it was only a matter of time before Rowan's *Shimmer* yarn (Lurex, basically) featured in some of my designs.

Shimmer is the opposite of *Kidsilk Haze* in every respect except attractiveness. It just lies down and shimmers, while the *Kidsilk* Haze gets all excitable and fluffy. This pattern is a variation on the old "pull-up" or quilt-stitch technique (which can be unattractive if worked in the wrong yarn). But in these two yarns with their competing yet complementary characters, it is lovely. It looks old-fashioned and modern all at once. You can see the *Shimmer* gleaming happily away on the surface of the smoky *Kidsilk Haze*, and the off-set pulled-up stitches look like shining mermaid scales with a surface lace texture overlaid on the mohair.

Although it looks rather complicated, once knitted up it really is easy, so it makes you look—and feel—very clever. A 12-row repeat may sound a bit intimidating but in fact eight of these rows are stockinette stitch, and a couple of the other rows involve a few slipped stitches, so it is easier than it sounds.

As well as the smoky gray and pewter version, I've also shown you a variation in cream *Kidsilk Haze* with silver *Shimmer*; this would make such a pretty warm stole for a wintry wedding day.

SKILL LEVEL
Easy to intermediate

SIZE OF STOLE
The finished stole measures approximately 64¼in/163cm long by 15in/38cm wide.

YOU WILL NEED
For the gray stole:

Yarn A   3 x ⁷/₈oz/25g balls of *Rowan Kidsilk Haze* in gray (Smoke, 605)

Yarn B   1 x ⁷/₈oz/25g ball of *Rowan Shimmer* in pewter (Anthracite, 094)

For the cream stole:

Yarn A   3 x ⁷/₈oz/25g balls of *Rowan Kidsilk Haze* in cream (Cream, 634)

Yarn B   1 x ⁷/₈oz/25g ball of *Rowan Shimmer* in silver (Silver, 092)

Pair of size 6 (4mm) needles

GAUGE
25 sts and 36 rows to 4in/10cm square measured over patt using size 6 (4mm) needles *or needle size necessary to obtain correct gauge.*

SPECIAL ABBREVIATIONS
Pu1tbl Pull up loop. With the right-hand needle, pick up the loop of *Shimmer* lying 4 rows below and slip it onto the left-hand needle. Now knit this, plus the next stitch (which will be in *Kidsilk Haze*) on the left-hand needle, together through the backs of the loops.

See also page 116.

ALISON'S TIPS
● The *Shimmer* tends to bunch together when cast on, so count and re-count to be sure you are not counting as one stitch two stitches that have just become very close together!

● Carry the yarn not in use up the side. This will be the

Shimmer, so just twist it over the *Kidsilk Haze* as you need it to carry up, making sure not to pull it too tight, and it will look fine—and save you endless slippery sewing in.

- Don't pull the *Shimmer* too tight at the other end of the rows either—give it a bit of "slack" so the other side doesn't start to undulate.

- If you wish, vary the needle size to gain a more open effect, and vary the stitch count to make a narrower version. It's a 10-stitch repeat plus 7 sts.

TO MAKE STOLE

Using size 6 (4mm) needles and yarn B, cast on 97 sts using the thumb method (see page 12), loosely.

Change to yarn A.

Next row (RS) Knit.

Next row (WS) Knit.

These two rows form garter st border. Repeat last 2 rows once.

Foundation row (RS) Using yarn B, K6, sl 2, wyif, sl 1, wyib, sl 2, *K5, sl 2, wyif, sl 1, wyib, sl 2, rep from * to last 6 sts, K6.

Lace overlay pattern

Row 1 (WS) K6, sl 5, *K5, sl 5, rep from * to last 6 sts, K6.

Change to yarn A.

Rows 2 to 5 Beg with a RS (K) row, work 4 rows in st st.

Change to yarn B.

Row 6 (RS) K1, sl 2, wyif, sl 1, wyib, sl 2, *K2, Pu1tbl, K2, sl 2, wyif, sl 1, wyib, sl 2, rep from * to last st, K1.

Row 7 (WS) K1, sl 5, *K5, sl 5, rep from * to last st, K1.

Change to yarn A.

Rows 8 to 11 Beg with a RS (K) row, work 4 rows in st st.

Change to yarn B.

Row 12 (RS) K3, Pu1tbl, *K2, sl 2, wyif, sl1, wyib, sl 2, K2, Pu1tbl, rep from * to last 3 sts, K3.

These 12 rows form overlay lace patt.

Cont in patt until stole measures approx. 63¾in/162cm and ending with patt Row 6 or 12.

Change to yarn A.

Next row (WS) Knit.

Next row (RS) Knit.

Rep these 2 rows once.

Change to yarn B.

Next row With WS facing, bind off knitwise.

TO FINISH

Sew in ends. With WS facing up, block the stole by pinning it to an ironing board or table, taking care to ease the sides straight. Refer to ball bands on both yarns for pressing advice. Using a slightly damp cloth, hover iron over the cloth. Remove cloth. Allow the stole to dry fully before unpinning.

hearts and flowers pillow

Kid Classic is a lovely companion for *Kidsilk Haze* and this pillow combines them. The front of the pillow is knitted in *Kid Classic,* and *Kidsilk Haze* is used in three shades to knit a little garden of roses, strewn around the central heart lace motif. I used leftovers for the flowers and you could use several toning shades, as I did.

The heart, the lace element in this design, is easy to follow and has the added bonus of some twinkly beads. To show the heart off, back the central part of the pillow with a vibrant contrasting fabric, and use this for the back of the pillow. I chose an inexpensive, satinized cotton in hot pink to glow through the filigree heart.

This design suits my style, as I love combining crafts: a bit of easy knitting, some beads to add sparkle, a very simple lace chart, and some simple sewing, hand or machine. Altogether it makes a very satisfying weekend project.

A set of three of these heart pillows in toning shades would be lovely, too.

SKILL LEVEL
Easy

SIZE OF PILLOW COVER
The finished pillow cover measures approximately
17in/43cm square.

YOU WILL NEED
Yarn A   2 x 1¾oz/50g balls Rowan *Kid Classic* in dark wine
red (Crushed Velvet, 825)
Oddments of Rowan *Kidsilk Haze*:
Yarn B   in hot pink (Candy Girl, 606)
Yarn C   in mid-pink (Blushes, 583)
Yarn D   in deep red (Liqueur, 595)
Note The ten flowers use three-quarters of a ball of *Kidsilk
Haze* in total.
Pair of size 7 (4.5mm) needles
Pair of size 5 (3.75mm) needles
Pillow form, 17¾in/45cm square
Piece of fabric, 18⅛in/47cm square (for the back)
Piece of matching fabric, 9½in/24cm square (to back the
heart motif)
Matching sewing thread
90 crystal beads (Size 6 seed beads)—40 for the heart and
50 for the centers of the roses

GAUGE
19 sts and 23 rows to 4in/10cm square measured over
stockinette st (unstretched) using yarn A and size 7 (4.5mm)
needles *or needle size necessary to obtain correct gauge.*

SPECIAL ABBREVIATIONS
bead 1 Place bead (see page 16).
See also page 116.

ALISON'S TIPS
● The fabric backing for the lace heart needs to be big
enough to cover the area of lace, when the pillow front is
stretched over the pillow form. If your fabric has a right side
and a wrong side, make sure the side that you want to be
facing outward backs the heart design.
● Don't try to sew the fabric backing directly onto the
wrong side of the knitted front: it will distort the gauge.

KEY
☐ K on RS, P on WS
■ bead
⊠ yfwd
⊘ K2tog

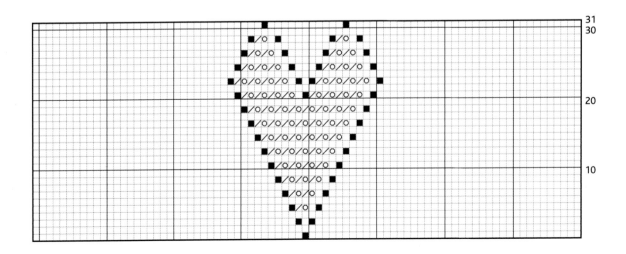

TO MAKE FRONT

Thread 40 beads onto yarn A (see page 16 for instructions on threading and beading).

With size 7 (4.5mm) needles and yarn A, cast on 81 sts using the thumb method (see page 12).

Row 1 Knit.

Row 2 Purl.

These two rows form st st.

Work in st st for 32 more rows.

Now work in patt from Chart.

Row 1 (RS) K40, bead 1, K40.

Row 2 and all WS rows Purl.

Row 3 K39, bead 1, K1, bead 1, K39.

Row 5 K38, bead 1, K1, yfwd, K2tog, bead 1, K38.

Cont as set, working from chart, until 31 rows have been worked and heart is complete.

Cont in st st for a further 33 rows.

Bind off.

TO FINISH FRONT

Sew in ends. With WS facing, pin the pillow front to your pressing surface. Referring to ball bands for instructions, very lightly press the pillow front, using a slightly damp cloth, a cool iron, and taking care not to press down at all. Let dry fully before unpinning.

TO MAKE ROSES (make 10)

With size 5 (3.75mm) needles and yarn B held single, cast on 66 sts using the lace cast-on method (see page 14).

Change to yarn C.

Row 1 (RS) *K4, K2tog, rep from * to end. *55 sts.*

Row 2 (WS) Purl.

Row 3 *K3, K2tog, rep from * to end. *44 sts.*

Change to yarn D.

Row 4 Purl.

Row 5 *K2, K2tog, rep from * to end. *33 sts.*

Row 6 Purl.

Row 7 *K1, K2tog, rep from * to end. *22 sts.*

Do not bind off. Cut yarn leaving a 6in/15cm tail. Thread yarn onto a yarn needle and pass needle and thread through all sts on needle, pushing them off the knitting needle as you thread through. Pull yarn up tight and sew firmly to secure flower shape. Sew in ends.

TO FINISH

Drape knitted front over pillow form and stretch it out slightly. Place flowers around heart in chosen positions (using photograph as guide) and pin in place. Sew flowers in place, stitching a group of five crystal beads into center of each flower as you secure them.

Fold over and press a ½in/1cm allowance on each side of smaller piece of fabric and neaten. Slip stitch onto one side of the pillow form. (This fabric shows through the lace heart, so must be placed accordingly.)

Fold over and press down a ½in/1cm allowance on each side of larger piece of fabric and neaten. With right sides together, sew larger piece of fabric to three sides only of pillow front using backstitch (if stitching by hand) or straight stitch (on a machine). Turn right sides out. Insert pillow form. Stitch fourth side by hand using overcasting stitch.

Finally, fluff up the roses and await Valentine's Day!

confection bed socks

This is a simple pattern for a pair of lacy bed socks, the sort of socks that will make you feel lovely, however cold it is. As I write this pattern and knit the socks, it's bitterly cold outside and has been for some weeks, which is what inspired me to knit these fast and easy socks. I won't wear them in bed, but instead I will pose shamelessly, modeling my new socks on the foot stool so I (and any family or guests) can gaze in awe at them. Because they are, quite simply, gorgeous.

I have combined two luscious pinks, one sweet and pale, one deep and rich. Together, they look fabulous. The shades are knitted together, giving the blended effect I was after. If you wanted these in one shade, then just use two ends of the same yarn.

The picot topping is just in one shade for contrast and then the whole confection is finished with narrow silk ribbons. Given how little time and yarn they take, I can see me making several pairs of these socks as gifts—or for myself, as I can think of at least four more color combinations of *Kidsilk Haze* that I want to try.

They are knitted flat, so there will be no heel-turning anxiety to cast a shadow over your knitting pleasure. The only shaping is at the toe and this is simple decreasing across the right-side rows. Then you neatly seam them up the back. Off the foot, they don't look so great, I admit, because they are shapeless, but once on, all is well and they mold to your foot.

SKILL LEVEL
Easy

SIZE OF SOCKS
The finished socks measure approximately 14in/37cm long, from picot edge to toe and 10½in/26cm around foot.

YOU WILL NEED
Yarn A   1 x ⁷/₈oz/25g ball of Rowan *Kidsilk Haze* in pale pink (Flower, 643)

Yarn B   1 x ⁷/₈oz/25g ball of Rowan *Kidsilk Haze* in deep red (Liqueur, 595)

Pair of size 3 (3.25mm) needles

Pair of size 6 (4mm) needles

Approximately 2¼yd/2.05m narrow satin or silk ribbon in matching or contrasting shade

GAUGE
17 sts and 24 rows to 4in/10cm square measured over lace patt with yarns A and B held together and size 6 (4mm) needles *or needle size necessary to obtain correct gauge.*

SPECIAL ABBREVIATIONS
s2kpo Slip next 2 sts as if to knit them tog, k1, then psso (2 sts decreased).

See also page 116.

PATTERN NOTES
Yarn is held DOUBLE throughout.

The top of the sock, including the picot hem and the eyelet row, is knitted with yarn A (held double).

The lace patt is a multiple of 6 sts plus 5, over a 4-row repeat. The number of sts here fits an average foot, like mine, with plenty of room for wiggling the toes! If you want them tighter or need to adapt the pattern for another size of foot width (such as a child's foot), subtract 6 sts, for example, and also reduce the length by omitting some of the 4-row repeats.

TO MAKE SOCKS (make 2)
Using size 3 (3.25mm) needles and yarn A, held double, cast on 41 sts, using the thumb or cable method (see pages 12 and 13).

Beg with a K row, work 4 rows in st st.

Row 5 (picot row) K2, *yfwd, K2tog, rep from * to last st, K1.

Beg with a purl row, work 6 rows in st st.

Change to size 6 (4mm) needles and work 2 further rows in st st.

Row 14 (WS, eyelet row) P3, *yrn, P2tog, rep from * to last 2 sts, P2.

Work 2 rows in st st.

Drop 1 strand of yarn A and pick up 1 strand of yarn B (so you are knitting with 1 strand of each shade).

Lace pattern
Row 1 (RS) K4, *yfwd, s2kpo, yfwd, K3, rep from * to last st, K1.

Row 2 Purl.

Row 3 K1, *yfwd, s2kpo, yfwd K3, rep from * to last 4 sts, yfwd, s2kpo, yfwd, K1.

Row 4 Purl.

(These 4 rows form lace pattern.)

Cont in patt until you have worked 11¾in/30cm of the lace patt (or to suit your foot length).

Shape toe
Work in st st, beg with a K row.

Toe Row 1 (RS) K4, *K2tog, K6, rep from * to last 5 sts, K2tog, K3. *36 sts.*

Toe Row 2 (and all foll WS rows) Purl.

Toe Row 3 K3, *K2tog, K5, rep from * to last 5 sts, K2tog, K3. *31 sts.*

Toe Row 5 K2, *K2tog, K4, rep from * to last 5 sts, K2tog, K3. *26 sts.*

Toe Row 7 K1, *K2tog, K3, rep from * to last 5 sts, K2tog, K3. *21 sts.*

Toe Row 9 *K2tog, K2, rep from * to last 5 sts, K2tog, K3. *16 sts.*

Toe Row 10 Purl.

Break yarn but leave a long tail. Thread tail onto a wool

needle and thread through remaining 16 "live" sts. Draw up
to close and secure by sewing end.

TO FINISH

Do not press.

With RS facing, join center back seam. Fold over picot edging
to WS and neatly slip stitch into place. Beginning at front
center, thread ribbon through the eyelets.

Slip socks onto your feet, tie ribbons prettily, and adopt foot-
modeling pose with footstool, sofa, knitting, and cup of tea!

Lace knitting is often at its best when it's simple and this is my default setting with both lace and *Kidsilk Haze*. On the other hand, it is also very satisfying to knit a more challenging piece sometimes and using *Kidsilk Haze* transforms a traditional-looking circular shawl into an heirloom piece with a difference.

There are elements within this shawl that are both quite easy and rather difficult. The center is easy and fast: a generic spiral using short-row shaping. This is knitted first and then seamed up to form the circle. The border is knitted afterward, again using short-row shaping to make it curve, and sewn on once it is the right length. It is shaped so that it curves snugly around the circular middle section. Here is the challenging part, as the border pattern has no "resting" rows and for the first few repeats, or until you have mastered the measure of it, you may well need a quiet, well-lit room with the door locked, the children/dogs safely stashed somewhere out of earshot, the telephone disconnected... and whatever it takes to allow you to concentrate.

I hope I have not scared you off because it is very, very lovely with its soothing lace cables, "feather and fan" section, and pretty little pointy bits, and well worth the little bit of extra effort.

I think circular shawls are much nicer than triangular-shaped ones and love the idea of draping this, folded in half, over my shoulders: light as a feather yet so comforting and elegantly warm. When not being deployed looking lovely on your shoulders, it can grace a table or chair back with equal panache. Just don't let the cat near it!

No one would normally put a baby in *Kidsilk Haze*—far too warming—but if you knitted the pattern in a fine cream cashmere or silk-cotton blend yarn, it would make a gorgeous Christening shawl.

SKILL LEVEL
Challenging

SIZE OF SHAWL
The finished shawl measures approximately 142¹/₈in/361cm around the circumference; 45¼in/115cm across the diameter (widest part).

YOU WILL NEED
4 x ⁷/₈oz/25g balls of Rowan *Kidsilk Haze* in ice blue (Glacier, 640)
Pair of size 8 (5mm) needles
Cable needle

GAUGE
16 sts and 26 rows to 4in/10cm square measured over garter st with yarn single using size 8 (5mm) needles *or needle size necessary to obtain correct gauge.*

ABBREVIATIONS
See page 116.

PATTERN NOTES
Yarn is held SINGLE throughout.

When there are short rows (the rows that say "turn"), you will work on these stitches only for that part, working on all the stitches on the next row. It is the short rows that give the rounded shapes this piece needs.

On the border pattern, the number of stitches varies from row to row, beginning and ending at 52. I have given you the number of stitches left after turning that you ought to have for each turning row.

ALISON'S TIPS
• I urge you to try at least one repeat of the border in a test yarn—not *Kidsilk Haze*—maybe a fine wool, to get the measure of the lace.

• My pattern for the border gives you the number of repeats I had to do. You may find it helpful to work up to

about this number but then, without binding off or allowing any stitches to escape from your needle, ease the work around the center and even pin it into place (as I did) to see exactly how much further you will need to continue knitting.

• When you are at a point where the seam will allow a good match between the cast-on and bound-off edges, bind off. Line up the two seams for neatness.

• To block and press this piece, I used a large bed sheet on the dining-room carpet so I could pin it out in full, WS down, easing the points out and pinning each one of these into the place I wanted it. Then I lightly pressed it with a cool iron (taking care not to touch the carpet with the iron), without pressure and using a slightly damp cloth, leaving it on the floor until it was dry before unpinning. Don't overdo the pressing, especially on the border and the cables.

• I wrote down all my rows in my notebook and marked them off as I went; if I had to stop partway through a row, I noted where I was by writing down what I last did and what was next. Had I lost that notebook, I think my sanity would have gone with it!

TO MAKE SHAWL
Center section
Using size 8 (5mm) needles, cast on 7 sts, using thumb method (see page 12).
Row 1 Yo, [K1, yfwd] 6 times, K1. *14 sts.*
Row 2 (and all alt rows) Knit.
Row 3 Yo, [K2, yfwd] 6 times, K2. *21 sts.*
Row 5 Yo, [K3, yfwd] 6 times, K3. *28 sts.*
Row 7 Yo, [K4, yfwd] 6 times, K4. *35 sts.*
Cont as set, inc 7 sts on every alt row, until the row **yo, [K46, yfwd] 6 times, K46** has been worked. *329 sts.*
Next row Knit.
Bind off loosely (using a larger sized needle if needed to match cast-on gauge). Sew up seam using mattress or slip stitch.
Border
There will be short-row shaping in places throughout the patt in order to allow the work to curve.

Using size 8 (5mm) needles, with yarn held single, cast on 52 sts using lace cast-on method (see page 14).

Row 1 K3, [K2tog, yfwd, K2] 3 times, K2tog, K11, K2tog, [K2tog, yfwd, K2] 3 times, K2tog, [yfwd, K2tog] 4 times.

Row 2 P10, turn (leaving 39 sts unworked).

Row 3 K2tog, [yfwd, k2tog] 4 times (working on the 10 original sts).

Row 4 P8, [K2tog, yfwd, K2] 3 times, P13 [K2tog, yfwd, K2] 3 times, K3 (on this row, you work all across the row).

Row 5 K3, [K2tog, yfwd, K2] 3 times, [K2tog] twice, [yfwd, K1] 5 times, yfwd, [K2tog] 2 times, [K2tog, yfwd, K2] 3 times, K1, [yfwd, K2tog] 3 times, yfwd, K1.

Row 6 P9, [K2tog, yfwd, K2] 3 times, p15, [K2tog, yfwd, K2] 3 times, K3.

Row 7 K3, [K2tog, yfwd, K2] 3 times, K2tog, K11, K2tog, [K2tog, yfwd, K2] 3 times, K2, [yfwd, k2tog] 3 times, yfwd, K1.

Row 8 P10, [K2tog, yfwd, K2] 3 times, P12, turn (leaving 16 sts).

Row 9 K1, K2tog, [yfwd, K1] 5 times, yfwd, [K2tog] twice, [K2tog, yfwd, K2] 3 times, K3, [yfwd, K2tog] 3 times, yfwd, K1.

Row 10 P11, [K2tog, yfwd, K2] 3 times, P14, P2tog, [Ktog, yfwd, K2] 3 times, K3.

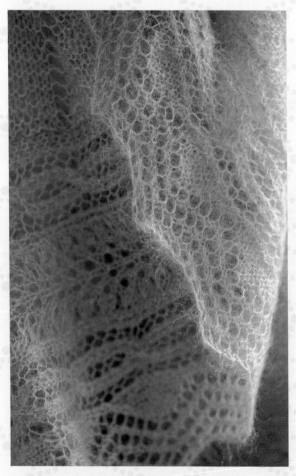

Row 11 K3, *K2tog, yfwd, K1, sl next 3 sts onto cable needle and leave at back of work, K1, K2tog, yfwd, K2 from cable needle, K next st on main needle AND last st on cable needle together, yfwd, K2, * K2tog, K11, K2tog, rep from * to * once, K4, [yfwd, K2tog] 3 times, yfwd, K1.

Row 12 P13, turn (leaving 39 sts).

Row 13 K6, [yfwd, K2tog] 3 times, yfwd, K1.

Row 14 *P13, [K2tog, yfwd, K2] 3 times, rep from * twice, K3.

Row 15 K3, [K2tog, yfwd, K2] 3 times, [K2tog] twice, [yfwd, K1] 5 times, yfwd, [K2tog] twice, [K2tog, yfwd, K2] 3 times, K3, K2tog, [yfwd, K2tog] 4 times.

Row 16 P12, [K2tog, yfwd, K2], 3 times, P15, [K2tog, yfwd, K2] 3 times, K3.

Row 17 K3, [K2tog, yfwd, K2] 3 times, K2tog, K11, K2tog, [K2tog, yfwd, K2] 3 times, K2, K2tog, [yfwd, K2tog] 4 times.

Row 18 P11, [K2tog, yfwd, K2] 3 times, P12, turn (leaving 16 sts).

Row 19 K1, K2tog, [yfwd, K1] 5 times, yfwd, [K2tog] twice, [K2tog, yfwd, K2] 3 times, K1, K2tog, [yfwd, K2tog] 4 times.

Row 20 P10, [K2tog, yfwd, K2] 3 times, P14, P2tog, [K2tog, yfwd, K2] 3 times, K3. *52 sts*

These 20 rows form border patt. Repeat 48 times more (49 in all). Bind off loosely.

Ease lace border around center, lining up the seams, and mattress or slip stitch into place. Block and press, referring to pattern notes and the ball band instructions.

cream puff pillow

In a rare example of restraint, I have used just one color, cream, for this pillow cover. Although this is not lace per se, I could not resist it, as I adore bobbles, and they are a similar type of textured stitch to lace, giving the pillow a romantic, slightly exotic look.

The *Cotton Glacé* yarn is smooth and firm and, because it is mercerized, it produces a knitted fabric with an attractive slight gloss. Adding bobble rows of fluffy *Kidsilk Haze* at intervals creates a storm of tiny snowballs to decorate it. Both yarns are knitted double, so the cotton knits up into a very firm (in fact, slightly stiff) base, and the *Kidsilk Haze* really needs to be held double to ensure the puffs stand up for themselves.

This is a decorative pillow and, being rather small, it is one for the front of your pillow-stack on the sofa, chair, or bed. I love making pillows and they fall into two categories: practical, but still lovely; or impractical and possibly even more lovely. This one belongs to the latter camp!

You could change the colors and use two closely toning shades (one for the main part, one for the bobbles). Or, you could go through your yarn stash and use leftover bits of *Kidsilk Haze*, and team it with, say, a black *Cotton Glacé*.

If you want to practice the bobbles, then why not make a festive greetings card for a special friend out of the samples? Add a small seed stitch border to a rectangle of cream *Cotton Glacé* and *Kidsilk Haze* puffs, use a fabric-friendly glue and a lovely thick card and, hey presto, you have created something personal and unique.

SKILL LEVEL
Easy

SIZE OF PILLOW COVER
The finished pillow cover measures approximately 11¾ x 11in/30 x 28cm.

YOU WILL NEED
Yarn A   3 x ⁷/₈oz/25g balls Rowan *Cotton Glacé* in cream (Ecru, 725). **Note** 5 balls if knitting the pillow back.

Yarn B   1 x ⁷/₈oz/25g ball Rowan *Kidsilk Haze* in cream (Cream, 634)

Pair of size 5 (3.75mm) needles

Piece of fabric to back pillow, 12⁵/₈in/32cm square (omit if you are knitting the back)

Pillow form, 11¾in/30cm square

Matching sewing thread

GAUGE
20 sts and 26 rows to 4in/10cm square measured over stockinette stitch, using Rowan *Cotton Glacé* held double and US size 5 (3.75mm) needles *or needle size necessary to obtain correct gauge.*

SPECIAL ABBREVIATIONS
MB Make bobble. Using yarn B held double, knit into the front, back, front, back, front, and back of the next stitch (6 stitches made); turn, P6; turn, K6, turn, [K2tog] 3 times; turn, P1, P2tog; turn, K2tog.
See also page 116.

ALISON'S TIPS
• You can carry the *Kidsilk Haze* along the back of the bobble rows, catching it in on every second or third stitch. You can also reduce the end-sewing to a minimum by carrying the *Kidsilk Haze* up the sides of the *Cotton Glacé* rows. In order to do this, you will first need to carry the *Kidsilk Haze* back along the row after placing the bobbles—on a WS row, just catch it along as you go and then leave it at the correct end ready to carry it up the side.

• Eliminate holes or gaps at the base of the puffs by first knitting firmly into the back of the stitch following the bobble AND by purling firmly into the back of the stitch on the other side of the bobble on the next (WS) row. I find that if you are carrying the *Kidsilk Haze* back on this purl row it really helps to tighten the bobbles up because you are able to give it an extra "tug" across the back of the bobble stitch.

• Don't block and press this item as the bobbles will be crushed. Instead, spray the front of the pillow cover lightly to just dampen it, then pin it out to size RIGHT SIDE UP. Then, using a pressing cloth, lightly press just the edges to aid sewing up. Leave uncovered, until dry.

• I backed my pillow with simple cream fabric. If you prefer a knitted back, buy 5 balls of yarn and knit it plain.

TO MAKE COVER FRONT
Using size 5 (3.75mm) needles and yarn A, held double, cast on 60 sts using the thumb method (see page 12).
Beg with a K row (RS), work 4 rows in st st.
Now work bobble patt.
Bobble Row 1 (RS) *Using yarn A, K7, change to yarn B, MB, rep from * to last 4 sts, K4.
Work 7 rows in st st using yarn A.
Bobble Row 2 Using yarn A, K3, *change to yarn B, MB, change to yarn A, K7, rep from * to last 9 sts, change to yarn B, MB, change to yarn A, K8.
Work 7 rows in st st using yarn A.
Cont as set in patt, alternating bobble Rows 1 and 2, with 7 rows of st st in between, until work measures approx. 10⁵/₈in/27cm, ending after a bobble row.
Work 5 rows in st st.
Bind off.
Sew in ends.
See Alison's Tips for notes on pressing pillow front.

TO FINISH
To make fabric back, press down a ⁵/₈in/1.5cm edge, folded to WS of fabric, and neaten. With RS together of knitted

front and fabric back, stitch knitted front to the fabric back around three sides. Turn RS out. Insert pillow form. Slip stitch the fourth side closed.

If you want to make a knitted back, using size 5 (3.75mm) needles and yarn A held double, cast on 60 sts. Starting with a knit row, work 11in/28cm in stockinette stitch. Bind off and sew in tail of yarn. To finish, following ball band instructions, block and press.

june flower stole

Two different—but quite easy—sections of lace are blended here, one of which is lightly beaded, the other adorned at each end with small creamy blossoms. Make as many or as few of the flowers as you wish, more is more in my opinion.

I have used a very small amount of soft mushroom-gray yarn to begin and end the stole and to trim the very edges of the flowers, just to give it a tiny contrast and lift, but by all means do it all in one shade. Should you use the contrast shade, you will need only a few ounces, so you may have some in your stash... I did.

I really love the frothy, flowery ends contrasted with the gently gleaming beaded eyelet section. Contrasts in lace work very well, I think. The main part has a narrow garter-stitch edge to help this essentially stockinette stitch section to lie down and behave.

Knitted in cream, it looks light and summery, and even hints at apple-blossom weddings. However, I would also like a sophisticated version in midnight blue, blackcurrant, or smoky gray.

SKILL LEVEL

Intermediate

SIZE OF STOLE

The finished stole measures approximately 53in/135cm long by 19in/48cm wide.

YOU WILL NEED

Yarn A   1 x ⁷/₈oz/25g ball Rowan *Kidsilk Haze* in soft gray (Majestic, 589)—approximately ¼oz/7g used

Yarn B   3 x ⁷/₈oz/25g balls Rowan *Kidsilk Haze* in cream (Cream, 634)

Pair of size 5 (3.75mm) needles

Pair of size 6 (4mm) needles

Approximately 310 silver beads (Size 6 seed beads)

GAUGE

19 sts and 26 rows knitted to 4in/10cm square measured over middle lace section pattern, when slightly stretched, using yarn A and size 6 (4mm) needles *or needle size necessary to obtain correct gauge.*

SPECIAL ABBREVIATIONS

bead 1 Place 1 bead (see page 16).

See also page 116.

TO MAKE STOLE

Using size 5 (3.75mm) needles and yarn A, cast on 91sts using lace cast-on method (see page 14).

Row 1 (RS, eyelet row) K1, *yfwd, K2tog, rep from * to end.

Row 2 Purl.

Change to yarn B.

Work end lace section as follows:

Row 1 (RS) K1, K2tog, yfwd, K1, yfwd, skpo, *K2, K2tog, yfwd, K1, yfwd, skpo, rep from * to last st, K1.

Row 2 *P2tog tbl, yrn, P3, yrn, p2tog, rep from * to end.

Row 3 K1, yfwd, skpo, K1, K2tog, yfwd, *K2, yfwd, skpo, K1, K2tog, yfwd, rep from * to last st, K1.

Row 4 P2, yrn, P3tog, yrn, *P4, yrn, P3tog, yrn, rep from * to

last 2 sts, P2.

These 4 rows form end lace section patt.

Rep Rows 1 to 4 until work measures 8in/20cm from cast-on edge, ending on Row 4.

Change to size 6 (4mm) needles.

Next row (RS) Purl.

Next row Knit.

Work middle lace section as follows:

Row 1 (RS) Knit.

Row 2 (and all WS rows) K3, purl to last 3 sts, K3.

Row 3 K7, yfwd, skpo, bead 1, K2tog, yfwd, K7, *yfwd, skpo, bead 1, K2tog, yfwd, k7, rep from * to end.

Row 5 K8, yfwd, sk2po, yfwd, *K9, yfwd, sk2po, yfwd, rep from * to last 8 sts, K8.

Row 7 Knit.

Row 9 K4, K2tog, yfwd, *K7, yfwd, skpo, bead 1, K2tog, yfwd, rep from * to last 13 sts, K7, yfwd, skpo, K4.

Row 11 K3, K2tog, yfwd, K9, *yfwd, sk2po, yfwd, K9, rep from * to last 5 sts, yfwd, skpo, K3.

Row 12 As Row 2.

These 12 rows form patt.

Repeat until stole measures 44½in/113cm from cast-on edge, ending with Row 12.

Next row (RS) Purl.

Next row Knit.

Change to size 5 (3.75mm) needles.

Work another section of border lace patt to match other end but finishing with Row 3.

Change to yarn A.

Next row (WS) Purl.

Next row (eyelet row) K1, *yfwd, K2tog, rep from * to end.

Bind off very loosely, knitwise, with WS facing.

TO FINISH

Sew in ends. Pin stole out on pressing surface, WS up, stretching gently, referring to ball bands for instructions, and using a damp pressing cloth, a cool iron, and no pressure, gently block and press. Let dry fully before unpinning.

Flowers (make 8)

Using size 5 (3.75mm) needles and yarn A and lace cast-on method (see page 14).

*Cast on 4 sts, bind off 2 sts, slip st on RH needle onto the LH needle, rep from * until 34 sts cast on.

Change to yarn B.

Row 1 (RS) Knit.

Row 2 Purl.

Row 3 Knit.

Row 4 *P2tog, rep from * to end. *17 sts*.

Row 5 K1, *K2tog, rep from * to end. *9 sts*.

Cut yarn leaving 6in/15cm tail. Thread tail onto a yarn needle and slip the 9 "live" sts off the knitting needle and onto and off the yarn needle; draw yarn to close the flower, spread it out and secure. Leave tail to sew flower onto stole.

Sew flowers as desired onto the end lace sections, sewing 2 clusters of 3 beads into the center of each flower.

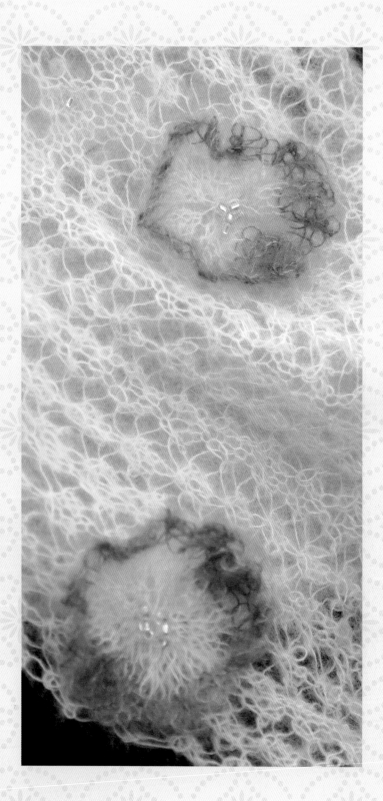

luster evening cape and corsage

This romantic evening cape has a deep lace border at the bottom, plus a gently flared, heavily beaded frill, finished with a picot bind-off. This little garment is very glamorous and a real pleasure to knit as well. A single layer of *Kidsilk Haze* over the shoulders is surprisingly cozy, so it's the perfect choice for a chilly evening when you want something to wear over your little black dress. As I wanted the beads to add a touch of drama and also some weight at the hem, I have placed them in bold clusters of threes. There was no way I would have made it through this book without at least one appearance of my beloved picot bind-off and it looks lovely here, bubbling along at the edges of the frill and collar.

The corsage is fairly quick and easy to knit, so use it to add a further touch of glamour to the cape or make it in some of the many shades of *Kidsilk Haze*. Bust into your stash by making a few, as each only takes a few ounces.

The little spirals tipped with crystal beads, rather like long stamens, are fun to knit. In fact, this corsage is a good lace practise-piece for first-time lace knitters—for a start, the gauge is not important. In this pattern, you are making the lace stitches on the purl rows.

SKILL LEVEL
Intermediate

SIZE OF CAPE
The finished cape measures 16¹/₈in/41cm from neck (excluding neck frill) to bottom edge, including bottom frill. Cape is approximately 63in/160cm wide above frill.

YOU WILL NEED
4 x ⁷/₈oz/25g balls of Rowan *Kidsilk Haze* in blue (Heavenly, 592)
Pair of size 8 (5mm) needles
Pair of size 6 (4mm) needles
Size 8 (5mm) circular needle or 31½in/80cm long circular needle (for the frills)
Approximately 735 crystal beads (Size 6 seed beads)

GAUGE
17sts and 22 rows to 4in/10cm square measured over lace pattern using yarn single and size 8 (5mm) needles, 19 sts and 24 rows to 4in/10cm measured over stockinette stitch using yarn single and size 8 (5mm) needles *or needle size necessary to obtain correct gauge.*

SPECIAL ABBREVIATIONS
bead 3 Place three beads together in a cluster (see page 16).
s2kpo Slip next 2 sts as if to knit them tog, K1, then psso (2 sts decreased).
See also page 116.

PATTERN NOTES
The cape is knitted with yarn held SINGLE but the corsage is knitted with yarn held DOUBLE.

When it comes to knitting the frills with beads, I have indicated that you ought to knit the main portion with the beads not threaded on, and then break your yarn and thread them on at the last minute. This will save wear on the yarn. There are almost 530 beads on the bottom frill alone. Normally I'd never put this many beads on any yarn, let alone *Kidsilk Haze*, but it's only for one row!

The beads are placed in the same way as normal (see page 16) but in this case you are making a cluster of 3 beads in one go. If you want single beads, divide the number by 3.

TO MAKE MAIN CAPE
Using size 8 (5mm) needles, cast on 301 sts with yarn single using the thumb or cable method (see pages 12 and 13), loosely.
Knit 1 row.
Lace section
Row 1 (WS) Purl.
Row 2 (RS) K1, *yfwd, K3, s2kpo K3, yfwd, K1, rep from * to end.
Row 3 Purl.
Row 4 P1, *K1, yfwd, K2, s2kpo, K2, yfwd, K1, P1, rep from * to end.
Row 5 K1, *P9, K1, rep from * to end.
Row 6 P1, *K2, yfwd, K1, s2kpo, K1, yfwd, K2, P1, rep from * to end.
Row 7 As Row 5.
Row 8 P1, *K3, yfwd, s2kpo, yfwd, K3, P1, rep from * to end.
These 8 rows form lace pattern.
Rep Rows 1 to 8 until cape measures approx. 7½in/19cm from cast-on edge, ending with Row 8.
Next row (WS) P10, P2tog, P10, P2tog, P to last 24 sts, P2tog, P10, P2tog, P to end. *297 sts.*
Next row (RS, dec) K16, *K2, K2tog, K5, K2tog, K17, rep from * to last st, K1. *277 sts.*
Cont in st st until work measures 8in/23cm ending with WS row.
Next row (dec) K16, *K1, K2tog, K5, K2tog, K16, rep from * to last st, K1. *257 sts.*
Cont in st st until work measures 12¼in/31cm, ending with WS row.
Next row (dec) K16, *K2tog, K5, K2tog, K15, rep from * to last st, K1. *237 sts.*
Work 3 rows in st st, thus ending with WS row.
Next row (dec) *K3 tog, rep from * to end. *79 sts.*

Change to size 6 (4mm) needles.

Work 5 further rows in st st beg with WS row.

Bind off loosely.

Front edge (both alike)

With size 6 (4mm) needles and RS facing, pick up and knit 70 sts (along side opening edge).

Knit 3 rows.

Bind off, very loosely.

TO FINISH

Sew in ends. Refer to ball band for pressing information.

Lightly press the cape, WS facing, using a slightly damp cloth

and a cool iron.

Neck frill

Using size 8 (5mm) needles, with RS facing, pick up and knit 128 sts evenly along bound-off edge, incl along the opening edges.

Next row (RS) Knit all sts.

Next row (WS) Purl all sts.

Next row *K1, K into front and back of next st, rep from * to end. *192 sts.*

Work 3 rows in st st.

Next row *K1, K into front and back of next st, rep from * to end. *288 sts.*

Next row Purl all sts.

Break yarn.

Thread 213 beads onto yarn.

Next row K2, *bead 3, K3, rep from * to last 2sts, bead 3, K1.

Next row Purl all sts.

Next row (picot bind-off) *Cast on 3 sts using lace method, bind off 6 sts; sl st on RH needle onto LH needle, rep from * to end.

Do not press.

Bottom frill

Using size 8 (5mm) circular needle with RS facing, pick up and knit 350 sts evenly along bottom cast-on edge.

Next row (WS) Purl all sts.

Next row (RS) *K1, K into front and back of next st, rep from * to end. *525 sts.*

Work 3 rows in st st.

Next row *K2, K into front and back of next st, rep from * to last st, K1. *700 sts.*

Work 3 rows in st st.

Break yarn.

Thread 522 beads onto yarn.

Next row K3, *bead 3, K3, rep from * to last st, K1.

Next row Purl all sts.

Next row (picot bind-off) *Cast on 3 sts using lace method, bind off 6 sts; sl st on RH needle onto LH needle, rep from * to end.

Do not press.

SKILL LEVEL
Easy

SIZE OF CORSAGE
The finished corsage measures 4³/₈in/11cm diameter; the long spiral is 6in/15cm; the short spiral is 4³/₈in/11cm.

YOU WILL NEED
1 x ⁷/₈oz/25g ball Rowan *Kidsilk Haze* in blue (Heavenly, 592)
Pair of size 3 (3.25mm) needles
Pair of size 6 (4mm) needles
10 crystal beads (Size 6 seed beads)

GAUGE
21 sts and 29 rows to 4in/10cm square measured over stockinette stitch using yarn single and size 6 (4mm) needles *or needle size necessary to obtain correct gauge.*

SPECIAL ABBREVIATIONS
M1pw Make 1 stitch purlwise. To make a stitch purlwise, the stitch before will always have been a purl stitch, so your yarn will be at the front of your work. Leaving the yarn at the front, and using the tip of the right-hand needle, lift the strand or bar of yarn visible between the needles onto the left-hand needle. Purl this strand of yarn as if it was a stitch, but do so through the back of the stitch (to prevent a hole forming).
See also page 116.

ALISON'S TIP
● When sewing on the spirals to the flower base, arrange them so they hang down over the seam on the base flower, effectively disguising it.

TO MAKE FLOWER BASE
Using size 6 (4mm) needles and yarn held single, cast on 27 sts using the thumb or cable method (see pages 12 and 13), leaving a 10in/25cm tail for sewing in at the end.
Row 1 (RS) K1, *P1, K1, rep from * to end.
Row 2 P1, *K1, P1, rep from * to end.
Row 3 K1, *P1, M1pw, K1, rep from * to end. *40 sts.*
Row 4 P1, *K2, P1, rep from * to end.
Row 5 K1, *P2, M1pw, K1, rep from * to end. *53 sts.*
Row 6 P1, *K3, P1, rep from * to end.
Row 7 K1, *P3, M1pw, K1, rep from * to end. *66 sts.*
Row 8 P1, *K4, P1, rep from * to end.
Row 9 K1, *P4, M1pw, K1, rep from * to end. *79 sts.*
Row 10 P1, *K5, P1, rep from * to end.
Row 11 K1, *P5, M1pw, K1, rep from * to end. *92 sts.*
Row 12 P1, *K6, P1, rep from * to end.
With RS facing, bind off purlwise, loosely.
Thread the cast-on tail through a yarn needle and run this through the cast-on edge. Draw up tight to close. With WS facing, use this thread to sew up the side seam, so the base flower lies flat. Do not press.

TO MAKE CENTER SPIRALS
Short spiral (make 1)
Using size 3 (3.25mm) needles and yarn held single, cast on 88 sts using the lace cast-on method (see page 14).
Row 1 *K2 tog, rep from * to end. *44 sts.*
Row 2 As Row 1. *22 sts.*
Bind off loosely.
Long spiral (make 1)
Using size 3 (3.25mm) needles, cast on 120 sts using the lace cast-on method.
Row 1 *K2 tog, rep from * to end. *60 sts.*
Row 2 As Row 1. *30 sts.*
Bind off loosely.
Sew in ends. Do not press.
Twist the spirals round your finger to make ringlets. Secure them to the center of the flower, and finish with two clusters of 5 beads at the center.

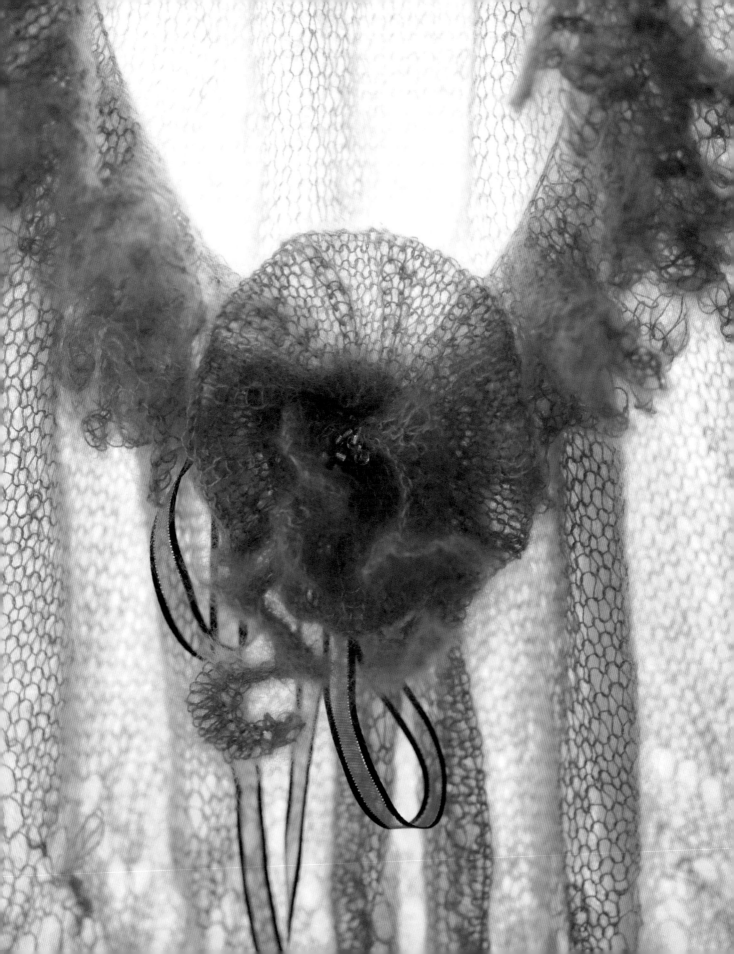

spiral shrug

This is a fairly substantial piece, an easy-to-wear and fun-to-knit shrug, with enough substance in the doubled-up *Kidsilk Haze* to keep you really cozy. But it is still light as a feather and rather lovely, too, with a great retro look. Tight, long cuffs contrast with airy lace in the main body and I used size 6 (4mm) needles on the sleeves to keep that part looser. It's long at the back of your waist, high at the back of your neck, and comes snugly around the sides. This hold-me-tight look is very flattering whether one is blessed with the 1940s-style curves or not. It also looks equally good when paired with jeans and a tight-fitting T-shirt or over a little black dress.

But the drama comes from the big, puffed, three-quarter length sleeves, ending with tight cuffs. I am a big fan of puffed sleeves because I think they make you look and feel so glamorous with all that lace wafting about. Being keen on baubles, bangles, and beads, I also like three-quarter length sleeves that show them off, but if you wanted yours down to the wrist, knit the cuff and the sleeve section a little longer before you change needle size—you may need more yarn.

An extra dimension to this is the subdued colorwash, in which I used warm gray teamed with a soft and gentle mauve. It drifts from mauve at the cuff to a mix of mauve and the warm gray at the start of the sleeves and settles into gray on its own for the most part. *Kidsilk Haze* does lend itself to this sort of colorwashing so you could choose your favorite shades and blend them, or do it in one shade only.

Finally, the stitch used is a trellis lace pattern, which, if you knit it flat, slopes gently and uniformly at the side edges.

SKILL LEVEL
Intermediate

SIZES OF SHRUG

	S	M	L	XL	
To fit bust					
	32–34	36–38	40–42	44–46	in
	81–86	91–97	102–107	112–117	cm
Measurements					
Depth of back (excluding body cuff)					
	22	22¾	23⅝	24⅜	in
	56	58	60	62	cm
Length (edge of cuff to cuff)					
	52¾	54¾	56¾	58¾	in
	134	139	144	149	cm

YOU WILL NEED
Yarn A   2 x ⁷/₈oz/25g balls of Rowan *Kidsilk Haze* in pale mauve (Dewberry, 600)

Yarn B   5 (6: 6: 7) x ⁷/₈oz/25g balls of Rowan *Kidsilk Haze* in soft gray (Majestic, 589)

Set of size 2 (2.5mm) double-pointed needles

Set of size 6 (4mm) double-pointed needles

Size 3 (3.25mm) circular needle or an 32–40in/80–100cm long circular needle

Stitch marker

GAUGE
23 sts and 32 rows to 4in/10cm square measured over twisted rib pattern, using yarn double and size 3 (3.25mm) needles; 21 sts and 32 rows to 4in/10cm square measured over spiral lace pattern, using yarn double and size 3 (3.25mm) needles *or needle size necessary to obtain correct gauge*.

ABBREVIATIONS
See page 116.

PATTERN NOTE
Yarn is held DOUBLE throughout.

ALISON'S TIPS
• I used short needles for the neat cuffs but quite long double-pointed needles for the main part. Use a circular needle if you prefer.

• If you like the pattern but want a more snug feel, try using the same stitch but holding one strand of *Kidsilk Haze* along with one of Rowan *Pure Wool 4 ply*; that would be really lovely too, and not too heavy. You may need to experiment with the needle sizes and swatch test it.

• I offer four sizes but to adjust the size of the shrug is easy by working fewer or more rows where indicated in the pattern. The opening section on the smallest size measures 22in/56cm across (44in/112cm all the way around). This part has to go right around you and under your arms. Pop your arm in and pull the sleeve up to three-quarter length and then measure the opening (flat) section, and when it reaches the other armpit without too much of a stretch, that's your width. Then, pick up and knit more stitches for the opening ribbed "cuff" section, finishing with an even number.

• If you are going to change the sleeve length, first make sure the stitches are not going to fall off the ends of the double-pointed needles by herding them into the middle of the needles, and then gently snuggle your arm into the sleeve as you go along to check for length.

TO MAKE SHRUG
Start at cuff edge.

Using size 2 (2.5mm) double-pointed needles and 2 strands of yarn A held together, cast on 50 (52: 54: 55) sts. Arrange on 3 needles, place a marker, and now work in rounds.

Knit one round.

Round 2 *K1tbl, P1*, rep to end of round.

Rep the last round for 3in/8cm.

Change to size 6 (4mm) double-pointed needles.

Next round *K into front and back of next st, rep from * to last st. *100 (104: 108: 110) sts.*

For small and extra large sizes only

Next round *K4, inc in next st, rep from * to end of round. *120 (132) sts.*

For medium and large sizes only

Next round K1 (2), *K4, inc in next st, rep from * to last 3 (6) sts, K these sts. *124 (128) sts.*

For all sizes

Beg lace spiral lace patt.

Round 1 * Yfwd, K2tog, rep from * to end.

Round 2 Knit.

These 2 rounds form spiral lace pattern.

Using 2 strands of yarn A, work the spiral lace patt for 2in/5cm.

Drop 1 strand of yarn A and join in 1 strand of yarn B.

Using 1 strand of yarn A and 1 strand of yarn B, work the spiral lace patt for 4¾in/12cm.

Drop rem strand of yarn A and join in 2nd strand of yarn B.

Using 2 strands of yarn B work the spiral lace patt for 3in/8cm.

Change to size 3 (3.25mm) double-pointed needles.

Cont until a total of 6¼ (6¾: 7: 7½)in/16 (17: 18: 19)cm have been worked using the 2 strands of yarn B, ending with a knit round.

(**Note** If you want to adjust sleeve length, add or subtract pairs of rounds at this point.)

Split for back opening.

Change to size 3 (3.25mm) circular needle.

Beg working back and forth in rows in lace patt on the circular size 3 (3.25mm) needle (i.e. you will get to the stitch marker at the end of the round and TURN, so start knitting flat, back and forth, noting that now Round 2 will become Row 2 and will be PURLED.)

You will notice your work now slopes diagonally as you knit. Continue working even in lace patt until back opening measures 22 (23¼: 24⅜: 25⅝)in/56 (59: 62: 65)cm along the edge, ending after Row 1.

(**Note** If you want to adjust the back width, add or subtract pairs of rows at this point.)

Change to size 3 (3.25mm) double-pointed needles, placing marker for beg of round. Beg working in the round as previously, cont to work in lace patt for 3⅛ (3½: 4: 4⅜)in/8 (9: 10: 11)cm or to match other sleeve if you have adjusted length.

Change to size 6 (4mm) double-pointed needles.

Cont as for first sleeve, reversing color changes until 2 rounds before cuff.

For small and extra large sizes only

Next round *K4, k2tog, rep from * to end of round. *100 (110) sts.*

For medium and large sizes only

Next round *K1 (2), *K4, K2tog, rep from * to last 3 (6) sts, K. *104 (108) sts.*

For all sizes

Next round *K2tog, rep from * to end of round. *50 (52: 54: 55) sts.*

Change to size 2 (2.5mm) double-pointed needles.

Round 1 *K1tbl, P1, rep from * to end.

Work in twisted rib, matching length to first sleeve cuff.

Knit one round.

Bind off.

Sew in ends. Refer to ball band for pressing instructions.

Lightly press the body of the shrug, avoiding the ribbed sleeve cuffs.

Body cuff

With size 3 (3.25mm) circular needle and using 2 strands of yarn B tog, RS facing, pick up and knit 260 (272: 286: 300) sts all around opening. Place marker.

(**Note** If you have adjusted length of back section, adjust number of sts accordingly, keeping to an even number).

Next round *K1tbl, P1, rep from * to end.

Cont for 3in/8cm.

Bind off loosely. Do not press garment.

Knitted in the round, this cowl is easy and quick to knit on a big circular needle, though you can use double-pointed needles if you prefer.

It looks as great pulled up over the back of the head on super-frosty days as it does snuggled round the neck or even pulled slightly down over one shoulder. It can be worn many different ways. Be careful not to cast on or bind off tightly or else it will not stretch so well. The lace pattern is a multiple of eight stitches, so you can go smaller (say, for a child) or larger, if you wish.

For this design, I wanted it to be comforting and snug. So I chose soft plum and raspberry for a warm winter look. I also knitted it in *Kidsilk Aura*, *Kidsilk Haze's* big double-knit sister, so it is very soft and warm. Having knitted it, I think a finer *Kidsilk Haze* version would be lovely, too. I'd be inclined to keep with the size 7 (4.5mm) needles to retain the looser finish. Beads, either knitted along the cast-on and bound-off edges, or crocheted on an edging afterward, would work well too, especially on a *Kidsilk Haze* version where they'd have a better chance to sparkle.

The *Kidsilk Aura* is DK weight and very, very fluffy, so it does not look as lacy as it might if you substituted, say, a luxury silk-wool DK blend, such as Rowan's *Silk Wool DK*, which I think would be beautifully smooth and drape well. However, this lace pattern knitted in *Kidsilk Aura* gives a subtle lacy texture and lots of loft and airiness.

SKILL LEVEL
Easy

SIZE OF COWL
The finished cowl measures 15in/38cm wide by 24¾in/63cm long; the circumference measures 30in/76cm.

YOU WILL NEED
Yarn A 3 x ⁷/₈oz/25g balls of Rowan *Kidsilk Aura* in dark pink (Damson, 762)

Yarn B 3 x ⁷/₈oz/25g balls of Rowan *Kidsilk Aura* in mid-pink (Raspberry, 756)

Size 7 (4.5mm) circular needle (or double-pointed needles)

Stitch marker

GAUGE
19sts and 24 rows to 4in/10cm square measured over rib pattern using size 7 (4.5mm) circular needle *or needle size necessary to obtain correct gauge.*

SPECIAL ABBREVIATIONS
tw2r Right twist: knit the next 2 sts tog, but do not slip sts from needle. Knit the first st again, then slip both sts from needle.

See also page 116.

PATTERN NOTE
When changing color, carry the yarn not in use up with you by twisting it over the working yarn at the marker point.

TO MAKE COWL
Using size 7 (4.5mm) circular needle and yarn A, cast on 144 sts using the thumb or cable cast-on method (see pages 12 and 13).

Join to knit in the round. Place marker.

Change to yarn B.

Rib round *K2, P2, rep from * to end.

Rep this round, which forms rib, until 2in/5cm have been worked.

Lace pattern
Rounds 1 to 4 are worked in yarn A, Rounds 5 to 8 in yarn B.

Round 1 *K1, tw2r, K1, P1, yo, skpo, P1, rep from * to end.

Rounds 2, 3, and 4 *K4, P1, K2, P1, rep from * to end.

Change to yarn B.

Round 5 *K1, tw2r, K1, P1, K2tog, yfrn, P1, rep from * to end.

Rounds 6, 7, and 8 *K4, P1, K2, P1, rep from * to end.

Work in patt, changing yarns every four rows as patt, until the cowl measures approx. 24in/57.5cm, ending with Round 4.

Change to yarn B.

Rep the rib round for 2in/5cm.

Change to yarn A.

Bind off loosely.

TO FINISH
Sew in ends. Turn cowl inside out and pin it out. Using a damp pressing cloth and cool iron, very lightly press the main section, avoiding the ribbing.

Let dry fully before unpinning.

This is the perfect, glamorous but warming evening accessory. It takes a modest amount of yarn and while it's not a weekend project, it is speedy for a little garment. Having three distinct sections—the lace rib cuffs, the main lace body, and the lacy bell-edging—also gives you achievable and satisfying goals.

The sleeves are elbow length ending with a sweet little ruffle that just brushes your forearm. The yarn is knitted single and there's plenty of airy waft. It feels as light as a feather but it really keeps you warm. A major bonus is that it doubles up as a short scarf, too. So, you can tuck it into your jacket *en route* to a party, and then, if it is coolish indoors, you can remove the jacket, unfurl the scarf, and slip on the shrug.

I love this soft amber shade but as it takes only two or three balls of yarn it would be hard to resist knitting it in other shades, too. The best bit of this garment is, of course, the lacy bell-edging which I *loved* knitting, holding it up to the light and swishing it about on the needles as I went along. I shall take this idea and use it in new ways, too: for example, in a double layer or in a different length, or to edge a plain or beaded scarf.

When choosing the right size, bear in mind that you need to leave a suitable gap when you sew it up. It doesn't actually go over your bust—it's your back and sides that are key to the sizing. Add row repeats to lengthen the arms and the span across the back and add stitch repeats to make it wider (further down your back).

SKILL LEVEL
Intermediate

SIZES OF SHRUG

	S	M	L	
To fit bust				
	32–34	36–38	38–40	in
	81–86	91–97	97–102	cm

Measurements

Depth of shrug

	12	13	14½	in
	30	33	37	cm

Width (cuff edge to cuff edge, excluding ruffle)

	40⅛	42½	44½	in
	102	108	113	cm

Ruffle

2in/5cm deep

YOU WILL NEED
2 (2: 3) x ⁷/₈oz/25g balls of Rowan *Kidsilk Haze* in golden yellow (Ember, 644)
Pair of size 3 (3.25mm) needles
Pair of size 5 (3.75mm) needles

GAUGE
24 stitches and 27 rows over 4in/10cm square measured over main lace pattern using size 5 (3.75mm) needles *or needle size necessary to obtain correct gauge.*

ABBREVIATIONS
See page 116.

PATTERN NOTES
Yarn is held SINGLE throughout.
The eyelet rib is a multiple of 4 sts plus 1 st over 6 rows.
The main body lace pattern is a multiple of 8 sts plus 1 st over 14 rows.
The ruffle is a multiple of 8 sts plus 7 sts over 16 rows.
When increasing is indicated, do this by knitting or purling into the front and back of the next stitch unless otherwise specified.
When decreasing is indicated, do this by knitting the next 2 sts together unless otherwise specified.

TO MAKE SHRUG
Using size 3 (3.25mm) needles, with yarn held single, cast on 73 (77: 81) sts using the thumb or cable cast-on method (see pages 12 and 13).

Lace rib

Row 1 (RS) K1, *P3, K1, rep from * to end.

Row 2 P1, *K3, P1, rep from * to end.

Row 3 As Row 1.

Row 4 As Row 2.

Row 5 K1, *P2tog, yo, P1, K1, rep from * to end.

Row 6 As Row 2.

These 6 rows form lace rib pattern.

Continue in lace rib until cuff measures 4³/₈in/11cm.

Change to size 5 (3.75mm) needles.

Next row (RS) Knit, increasing by 0 (4: 8) sts, evenly across the row. *73 (81: 89) sts.*

Next row Purl.

Main body lace pattern

Beg with RS row.

Rows 1 to 8 K1, *P1, K1, rep from * to end.

(These 8 rows are worked in seed st.)

Row 9 K1, *yfwd, skpo, K3, K2tog, yfwd, K1, rep from * to end.

Rows 10 and 12 Purl.

Row 11 *K2, yfwd, skpo, K1, K2tog, yfwd, K1, rep from * to last st, K1.

Row 13 *K3, yfwd, sk2po, yfwd, K2, rep from * to last st, K1.

Row 14 Purl.

These 14 rows form main body lace pattern. Cont until main lace section measures approx. 30¾ (32¾: 34⁵/₈)in/78 (83: 88)cm ending with Row 14.

Rep Rows 1 to 8.

Next row (RS) Knit, decreasing by 0 (4: 8) sts evenly across row. *73 (77: 81) sts.*

Next row Purl.

Change to size 3 (3.25mm) needles.

Work 4³/₈in/11cm in lace rib pattern.

Bind off.

With RS facing and using size 3 (3.25mm) needles, pick up and knit 71 (75: 80) sts. Next row P, increasing by 0 (4: 7) sts evenly across the row. *71 (79: 87) sts.*

Ruffle pattern

Row 1 (RS) P7, *K1, P7, rep from * to end.

Row 2 K7, *P1, K7, rep from * to end.

Row 3 P7, *yo, K1, yfrn, P7, rep from * to end.

Row 4 K7, *P2, P1tbl, K7, rep from * to end.

Row 5 P7, *yo, K3, yfrn, P7, rep from * to end.

Row 6 K7, *P4, P1tbl, K7, rep from * to end.

Row 7 P7, *yo, K5, yfrn, P7, rep from * to end.

Row 8 K7, *P6, P1tbl, K7, rep from * to end.

Row 9 P7, *yo, K7, yfrn, P7, rep from * to end.

Row 10 K7, *P8, P1tbl, K7, rep from * to end.

Row 11 P7, *yo, K9, yfrn, P7, rep from * to end.

Row 12 K7, *P10, P1tbl, K7, rep from * to end.

Row 13 P7, *yo, K11, yfrn, p7, rep from * to end.

Row 14 K7, *P12, P1tbl, K7, rep from * to end.

Row 15 P7, *yo, K13, yfrn, P7, rep from * to end.

Row 16 K7, *P14, P1tbl, K7, rep from * to end.

This completes ruffle pattern. Bind off loosely. Make another ruffle on the other end.

TO FINISH

Sew in ends. Refer to ball band for care instructions. With WS facing, pin shrug out. Using a damp pressing cloth and cool iron, very gently press garment by hovering iron over item, using no actual pressure. DO NOT press lace rib cuffs or ruffles. With RS facing tog, sew up shrug arms, including ruffles. The space you leave is the opening for the garment. You need it large enough to allow you to put it on easily but tight enough not to "flute" at the back. Baste it with contrasting thread and try on before stitching firmly. This is much easier than trying to undo *Kidsilk Haze* seams. For my own, I sewed up the ruffles, the rib, and almost two main body lace repeats.

This is a delicate, ethereal piece, which can be worn as decoration or tucked into the neck of your winter coat or jacket. "Stars" are knitted in opposing rows—simple gathered lace stitches forming an almost three-dimensional effect, knitted on over-sized needles. It's a simple repeat so you could just widen it or knit the yarn double on even bigger needles for even more of a snuggle—to make a sofa throw, for example. It's a repeat of 4 stitches plus 1.

For a scarf, you use just one ball of *Kidsilk Haze* in each shade. You can make it in a long weekend, so it is also a perfect gift for some lucky friend or relative. It's fairly easy lace too—far easier than it looks. I have graded it as easy to intermediate because honestly, once you have worked the Star stitch a few times, it is easy.

When dreaming about this little design, I swatched it first in one shade and then in the two you see here. In one shade, the "stars" show a little less brightly but still give a lovely effect. If you do go for the one shade, just one ball of *Kidsilk Haze* will still give you a scarf that is a useful length. You could also add beads in Rows 1 and/or 3. Beads are my one weakness, and I did a beaded swatch too, so the next time I knit this, it will be beaded!

SKILL LEVEL
Easy to intermediate

SIZE OF SCARF
The finished scarf measures 54½in/138cm long and approximately 11in/28cm wide.

YOU WILL NEED
Yarn A 1 x ⁷/₈oz/25g ball of Rowan *Kidsilk Haze* in soft gray (Majestic, 589)
Yarn B 1 x ⁷/₈oz/25g ball of Rowan *Kidsilk Haze* in cream (Cream, 634)
Pair of size 10 (6mm) needles

GAUGE
24 sts and 16 rows to 4in/10cm measured over lace patt (6 Star stitches and 6 purl stitches) using size 10 (6mm) needles *or needle size necessary to obtain correct gauge.*

SPECIAL ABBREVIATIONS
bead 1 Place bead (see page 16).
Str st Star stitch. Purl 3 sts together BUT DO NOT complete stitch; leave sts on the left-hand needle, then yo (see page 117), then needle back into the same three purl sts again, then complete the st, allowing the three purl sts to slip off the needle this time. (Three sts purled together but you still have three sts.) The number of sts on rows never varies in this patt.
See also page 116.

PATTERN NOTE
Yarn is held SINGLE throughout.

ALISON'S TIPS
• You can carry the yarns up the side but take care not to pull tight in any way as it is very easy to do this and make the scarf "bend" to one side; leave the yarns fairly slack.
• Purling three stitches together is easy because the needles are big, but it's harder if you have knitted tightly on the row before. Try to maintain a fairly relaxed gauge.
• When purling the three stitches together, give the work a firm tug downward to ease your needle in and use the shaft of the needle as well, not just the tip, to achieve the gauge. I gave my needle a little "wiggle" each time I worked this stitch to make sure I was on gauge and not tightening up (much to the annoyance once of a man on the train!).
• If you find the Star stitch tricky, practice it first using an easier yarn such as 4-ply cotton or wool.

TO MAKE SCARF
Using size 10 (6mm) needles and yarn A held single, cast on 57sts using the lace cast-on method (see page 14).
Rows 1 to 4 Knit.
These 4 rows form garter st border.
Change to yarn B.
Row 1 Knit.
Row 2 P1, *Str st, P1, rep from * to end.
Change to yarn A.
Row 3 Knit.
Row 4 P3, Str st, *P1, Str st, rep from * to last 3 sts, P3.
These 4 rows form Str st patt.
Cont in patt, alternating shades as set, ending after Row 2 and reserving enough yarn to work 4 rows of garter st.
Change to yarn A.
Work 4 rows of garter st.
Bind off loosely knitwise with WS facing to match look of the lace cast-on look. (If you find this difficult, use a larger needle.)

TO FINISH
Sew in ends. Referring to ball bands for instructions, with WS facing, pin out and lightly press. Let dry fully before unpinning.

This is a showy little pillow, knitted in toning shades of Rowan's *Fine Milk Cotton*, which is a 4-ply yarn, and *Kidsilk Haze*. I really love these cool shades and the contrasting natures of the yarns.

With this design, you get a double dose of lace because the pillow itself has a lacy overlay of *Kidsilk Haze*, plus the rather flamboyant, deep, pure lace edging. The *Kidsilk Haze* element of the pillow top is knitted in a slip-stitch design so it sits over the *Fine Milk Cotton*, which forms a basic stockinette stitch base. The lacy border is knitted separately and sewn around the edges.

My younger daughter said it was the sort of pillow that should be used to present something to a princess. A fabulous diamond, perhaps… ?

SKILL LEVEL
Intermediate

SIZE OF PILLOW
The finished pillow measures 10in/25cm square excluding lace border; the lace border measures 2¾in/7cm deep at widest point.

YOU WILL NEED
Yarn A   2 x 1¾oz/50g balls Rowan *Fine Milk Cotton* in very pale blue-green (Apple Pips, 482)

Yarn B   1 x 7/8oz/25g ball of Rowan *Kidsilk Haze* in mallard blue (Trance, 582)

Pair of size 3 (3.25mm) needles

Approximately 1¼oz/30g of batting (to stuff the pillow)

GAUGE
32 sts and 52 rows over 4in/10cm square measured over slip stitch pattern, with both yarns as indicated, using size 3 (3.25mm) needles *or needle size necessary to obtain correct gauge.*

SPECIAL ABBREVIATIONS
Pu1 Pull up 1 st. Insert point of RH needle upward under the loose strand of the slip sts three rows below and knit it together with the next st.

See also page 116.

TO MAKE FRONT AND BACK (knitted alike)
Using size 3 (3.25mm) needles and yarn A, cast on 81 sts using thumb method (see page 12).

Foundation row Knit.

Change to yarn B.

Row 1 (WS) P2, *wyib, sl 5, wyif, P1, rep from * to last st, P1.

Change to yarn A.

Row 2 Knit.

Row 3 Purl.

Change to yarn B.

Row 4 K1, sl 3, Pu1, *sl 5, Pu1, rep from * to last 4 sts, sl 3, K1.

Row 5 P1, wyib, sl 3, wyif, P1, *wyib, sl 5, wyif, P1, rep from * to last 4 sts, wyib, sl 3, wyif, P1.

Change to yarn A.

Row 6 Knit.

Row 7 Purl.

Change to yarn B.

Row 8 K1, Pu1, *sl 5, Pu1, rep from * to last st, K1.

These 8 rows form patt.

Repeat until front measures approx. 10in/25cm, ending on a Row 4 or 8. Change to yarn A and bind off purlwise.

Sew in ends and with WS facing, pin out and referring to ball bands, gently press with cool iron and damp pressing cloth.

TO MAKE LACE EDGING
Using size 3 (3.25mm) needles and yarn B held single, cast on 17 sts.

Row 1 (RS) K3, yfrn, P2tog, yrn, P2tog, yo, K1tbl, K2tog, P1, wyib, skpo, K1tbl, yfwd, K3.

Row 2 K3, P3, K1, P3, K2, yfrn, P2tog, yrn, P2tog, K1.

Row 3 As Row 1.

Row 4 As Row 2.

Row 5 K3, yfrn, P2tog, yrn, P2tog, yo, K1tbl, yfwd, K2tog, P1, wyib, skpo, yfwd, K4. *18 sts.*

Row 6 K4, P2, K1, P4, K2, yfrn, P2tog, yrn, P2tog, K1.

Row 7 K3, yfrn, P2tog, yrn, P2tog, yo, K1tb1, K1, K1tbl, yfwd, sk2po, yfwd, K5. *19 sts.*

Row 8 K5, P7, K2, yfrn, P2tog, yrn, P2tog, K1.

Row 9 K3, yfrn, P2tog, yrn, P2tog, yo, K1tbl, K3, K1tbl, yfwd, K7. *21 sts.*

Row 10 Bind off 4 sts (1 st remains on RH needle), K2, P7, K2, yfrn, P2tog, yrn, P2tog, K1. *17 sts.*

These 10 rows form patt.

Rep until the edge fits around all the sides of the pillow.

Bind off after Row 10.

TO FINISH
Refer to ball bands for care instructions. Pin the edging out, WS facing, making sure the points are fully pinned out.

Press using a damp pressing cloth and a cool iron. Hold the pillow front and back together with RS facing each other. Insert the lace border just inside the covers, with the flat edge to the edges of the pillow cover. Pin in place. Backstitch the covers together, trapping the lace border in between as you stitch. Ease the border around the corners so as not to distort the border once the pillow is laid flat. Stitch three sides together, then turn work to RS facing.

Stuff the pillow with just enough batting to make it plump but not overstuffed. Slip stitch the last side together and slip stitch the lace border in place. Neatly sew the cast-on and bound-off edges of the lace border together.

Place the pillow on your work surface, covered with a blocking cloth, and with WS (of lace border, as both sides of the actual pillow are the same), facing up, pin the border all around to the blocking cloth. With a damp pressing cloth and a cool iron, lightly press the border all around (taking care at the corners to make sure the border lies flat), and give the pillow itself a very gentle press. Let dry fully before unpinning.

avalon camisole

The simple lace-rib chevron design of this pretty camisole is quite easy and the gentle, rather modest, shaping is achieved by changing needle sizes to go in and out a little—not too much, I wanted it to look innocent, which I think it does. I also really like the way it feels like 1920s lingerie—only knitted in *Kidsilk Haze*.

Knitted double as this is, it's probably sturdy enough to wear on its own, but I think it looks best over a fine tank top or blouse and your oldest, most comfortable pair of jeans. If you want a more ethereal version, for which you would certainly need a tank top or camisole underneath, you could follow the pattern but use the yarn single.

The shoulder straps are knitted lengthwise, with what are essentially large buttonholes or eyelets to allow a ribbon to be threaded through. The ribbon keeps the top up and adds a lovely vintage feel, too, as do the small beaded roses that adorn the strap ends on the front.

The whole confection is finished with a very simple crochet border with clusters of beads sparkling around the top and bottom edges. For the really crochet-phobic, I suggest that you pick up and knit an edge with a longish circular needle, add the beads as on page 16 (but in groups of three at a time), work one more row in garter stitch, and bind off.

This pattern has reducing "ease" on the fit. In other words, it measures less than you do because it stretches. If you want an even more figure-hugging style, remove a couple of repeats from the lace stitch pattern. It is a 6-stitch repeat, plus 2 stitches.

SKILL LEVEL

Intermediate

SIZES OF CAMISOLE

S	M	L	XL	
To fit bust				
32–34	36–38	40–42	44–46	in
81–86	91–97	102–107	112–117	cm
Measurements				
Width of camisole				
30¾	35½	40	44¾	in
78	90	102	114	cm
Length (excluding straps)				
13¾	15	16¼	17½	in
35	38	41	44	cm

Straps

Approximately 12½in/32cm

YOU WILL NEED

4 (5: 6: 7) x ⁷⁄₈oz/25g balls of Rowan *Kidsilk Haze* in pale pink (Flower, 643)

Pair of size 6 (4mm) knitting needles

Pair of size 5 (3.75mm) knitting needles

Pair of size 4 (3.5mm) knitting needles

Size 6 (4mm) crochet hook

Approximately 27½in/70cm ribbon, 1in/2.5cm wide

Approximately 200 (250: 250: 300) crystal beads (Size 6 seed beads)

GAUGE

20 sts and 28 rows to 4in/10cm square measured over lace patt using yarn double and size 6 (4mm) needles *or needle size necessary to obtain correct gauge.*

ABBREVIATIONS

See page 116.

TO MAKE CAMISOLE (make 2 parts alike)

With size 6 (4mm) needles and yarn held double, cast on 78 (90: 102: 114) sts using the thumb method (see page 12).

Row 1 (RS) K2, * P2, K2; rep from * to end.

Row 2 P2, * K2, P2; rep from * to end.

These 2 rows form rib patt.

Work in rib until bottom rib measures approx.

2 (2¼: 2½: 2¾)in/5 (5.5: 6: 6.5)cm, ending with Row 2, and increasing 2 sts across last row. *80 (92: 104: 116) sts.*

Commence lace pattern.

Row 1 (RS) P2, *yo, skpo, K2tog, yfrn, P2, rep from * to end.

Row 2 K2, *P4, K2, rep from * to end.

Row 3 P2, *K4, P2, rep from * to end.

Row 4 As Row 2.

These 4 rows form lace patt.

Work lace patt rows 4 (4: 5: 5) times more.

Change to size 5 (3.75mm) needles.

Work lace patt rows 3 (4: 5: 5) times more.

Change to size 4 (3.5mm) needles.

Work lace patt rows 4 (4: 4: 5) times more.

Note If you are long waisted, add a row repeat here.

Change to size 5 (3.75mm) needles.

Work lace patt rows 3 (4: 4: 5) times more.

Change to size 6 (4mm) needles. Work lace patt rows 4 (4: 5: 5) times more, dec 2 sts evenly across last row. *78 (90: 102: 114) sts.*

Change to size 4 (3.5mm) needles.

Work the rib patt (at the start) for 1¼in/3cm.

Bind off.

TO FINISH CAMISOLE

Sew in ends. Refer to ball band for care instructions.

With WS facing, pin out camisole front and back. Using a damp pressing cloth and a cool iron, very lightly press the work, omitting the ribbing at the top and bottom. Let dry.

With RS facing, sew front and back tog, using backstitch or mattress stitch.

STRAPS (make 2)

Using size 6 (4mm) needles and yarn held double, cast on 8 sts using thumb method (see page 12).

Beg with a RS row, work 4 rows in garter st.

Next row K2, bind off 4, K1.

Next row K2, turn and (using the lace cast-on method, see page 14) cast on 4 sts, turn, K2.

These last 2 rows form the "eyelets" through which to thread the ribbon.

Work these two eyelet rows after every four rows of garter st until straps measure required length (less approx. ½in/1cm). I worked 16 (17: 18: 19) eyelets according to size.

Work a further 4 rows of garter st.

Bind off.

TO FINISH

Sew in ends. Press as above.

Thread the ribbon through the "eyelets." Turn and neatly hem and sew the ribbon to the straps at each end. Pin the straps inside the camisole and firmly sew into place.

ROSES (make 2)

Using size 4 (3.5mm) needles, yarn held single, and the lace cast-on method (see page 14), *cast on 4 sts, bind off 2 sts, slip st from RH needle onto LH needle, rep from * until 34 sts cast on. This forms the picot-edge cast on.

Next row (RS) Knit.

Next row Purl.

Next row Knit.

Next row P2tog across row. *17 sts.*

Next row K1, *K2tog, rep from * to end. *9 sts.*

Cut yarn leaving a 8in/20cm tail. Do not bind off. Thread tail onto a yarn needle and thread the "live" sts onto and then off the yarn needle. Draw firmly to close the center of the flower and secure with a few sts. Sew each flower to the front of the camisole at the point where the straps meet the body (using photograph as guide), securing each in place with two clusters of three beads.

CROCHET EDGING

(This beaded crochet edging to the top and bottom of the camisole has slightly fewer crochet sts and beads for the top, as it is narrower than the bottom.)

Thread approx. 100 (125: 125: 150) beads onto yarn (see page 16), held double.

Using size 6 (4mm) crochet hook, work a crochet border evenly around the wrong side of camisole cast-on edge:

Round 1 (WS) Join yarn with a slip st to cast-on edge of knitted border, work 1ch, *1sc, slide 3 beads up close to RS of work, and, keeping beads in position together, work 1sc to secure bead cluster, 1ch, 1sc, 1ch, rep from * to end of round, join with a slip st to first sc of round.

Fasten off.

Repeat for bound-off edge.

Sew in any ends. No pressing required.

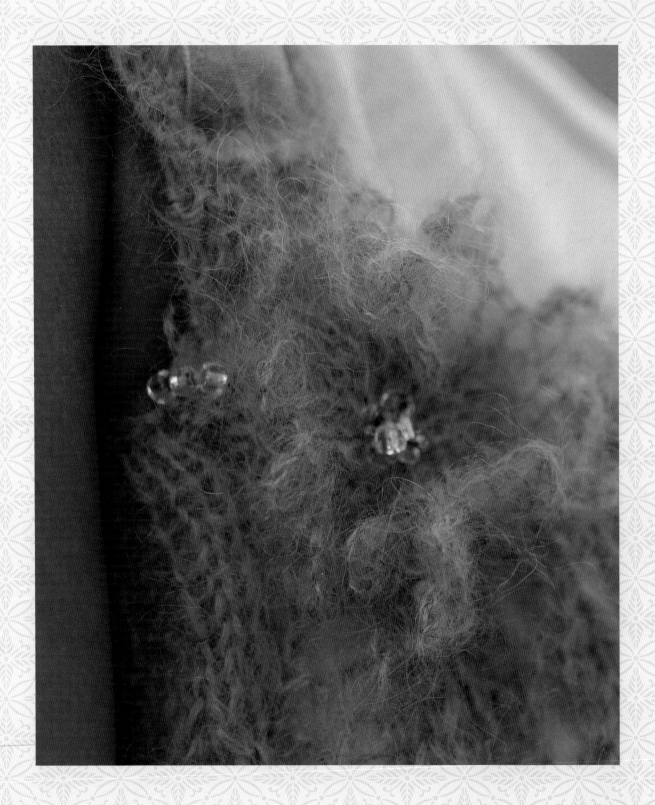

dream evening bag

With sparkly things being my one weakness, this bag is a favorite. By adding so many sequins and beads, I have literally doubled the weight of the yarn! It feels opulent and rich, and it certainly makes a statement.

The lace is the icing on the cake. At the start, you knit a deep lace border that folds back over the top of the bag. This is also beaded and here the yarn is held single. Then the main section is given over to stockinette stitch, with yarn held double, and the glitter begins. A wide organza ribbon is woven through the eyelets and forms the handle. The bag is lined with a gray silk (the lining shows through very slightly, despite the sides being knitted double and encrusted with jewels, so bear that in mind).

I notice when I teach workshops that almost everyone loves knitting with beads. However, knitting with sequins is not as popular. In fact, I have known students quit after only two rows and go back to beads. That's fine, I don't mind in the least. What I will say, if the 1,000 beads plus 1,000 sequins scares you, is this: like all fiddly knitting tricks, this is pesky for a few rows, then it speeds up, then it gets a bit tedious toward the end. If the sequins are overwhelming, just knit the beads in on their own.

SKILL LEVEL
Intermediate

SIZE OF BAG
The finished bag measures approximately 8¾in/22cm square excluding the lace border, which measures 2¾in/7cm at deepest point.

YOU WILL NEED
2 x ⅞oz/25g balls of Rowan *Kidsilk Haze* in cream (Cream, 634)
Pair of size 6 (4mm) needles
Piece of lining fabric, approximately 8 x18in/20 x 45cm
48in/122cm of silk ribbon, 1½in/3.5cm wide
Approximately 1,000 silver beads (Size 6 seed beads)
Approximately 1,000 silver sequins, ⅜in/10mm wide
Matching sewing thread

GAUGE
20 sts and 32 rows to 4in/10cm square measured over bead and sequin pattern, using yarn held double and size 6 (4mm) needles *or needle size necessary to obtain correct gauge.* However, gauge is not crucial with this item.

SPECIAL ABBREVIATIONS
bead 3 Place 3 beads together (see page 16).
BS1 Place a bead and sequin together (see page 16).
See also page 116.

PATTERN NOTES
The sts worked tbl are NOT knitted together, but one at a time.
The technique for threading and knitting the bead-plus-sequin together is the same as for beads on their own (see page 16). Note, however, that whatever you thread onto your yarn LAST, comes off the yarn FIRST. So you must start threading with a bead and end with a sequin: bead, sequin, bead, sequin, and so on.
The beads and sequins for the main part are threaded onto yarn held DOUBLE; the beads for the lace section are threaded onto yarn held SINGLE.

ALISON'S TIPS
- As this uses a lot of beads and sequins, don't thread 500 plus on each ball at once. I put only a couple of hundred on at a time, because they really wear the yarn and your patience when you have to keep moving them down the yarn every few minutes.
- Use a long, fine sewing needle to thread the beads and sequins (making sure that the beads and the sequins will pass over this needle). Put the beads on one side of you, on a piece of plush fabric to stop them rolling about, and the sequins next to them, in a flat saucer, so you can achieve a rhythm.

TO MAKE BAG (make two sides)
First thread 33 beads onto yarn.
Using size 6 (4mm) needles with yarn held single, cast on 45 sts using lace cast-on method (see page 14).
Row 1 (RS) *K3, bead 3, rep from * to last st, K1.
Row 2 P22, P2tog, P to end. *44 sts.*
Lace top
Row 1 (RS) *Skpo, [K1tbl] 3 times, yfwd, K1, yfwd, [K1tbl] 3 times, K2tog, rep from * to end.
Rows 2, 4, 6, and 8 Purl.
Row 3 *Skpo, [K1tbl] twice, yfwd, K1, yfwd, skpo, yfwd, [K1tbl] twice, K2tog, rep from * to end.
Row 5 *Skpo, K1tbl, yfwd, K1, [yfwd, skpo] twice, yfwd, K1tbl, K2tog, rep from * to end.
Row 7 *Skpo, yfwd, K1, [yfwd, skpo] 3 times, yfwd, K2tog, rep from* to end.
Row 9 *K1, P1, K7, P1, K1, rep from * to end.
Row 10 *P1, K1, P7, K1, P1, rep from * to end.
These 10 rows form pattern.
Repeat the last 10 rows once more.
Break yarn. From now on, yarn is held double.
Thread on beads and sequins to double yarn (referring to note above on threading them on in the right order).
Note A 4-row rep takes 21 beads and sequins (2 beaded/

sequinned rows and 2 purl rows in between).

Next row Purl (to form fold line).

Row 1 (WS) Purl.

Row 2 (RS) Knit.

These 2 rows form st st.

Work a further 5 rows in st st.

Row 8 (RS, eyelet row) K3, *bind off 3, K next 3 sts, rep from * to last 6 sts, bind off 3, K2 rem st.

Row 9 P3, *cast on 3, K4, rep from * to last 6 sts, cast on 3, K3.

Row 10 K22, K into front and back of next st, K to end. *45 sts.*

Commence bead and sequin pattern.

Row 1 (RS) K2, BS1, *K3, BS1, rep from * to last 2 sts, K2.

Row 2 Purl.

Row 3 K4, BS1, *K3, BS1, rep from * to last 4 sts, K4.

Row 4 Purl.

These 4 rows form bead and sequin section.

Repeat until bag measures approx. 7½in/19cm from eyelet row.

Work 2 rows in st st. Bind off.

TO FINISH

Refer to ball band for care instructions. With WS facing, pin bag to base cloth. With a damp pressing cloth and a cool iron, hover the iron over the work—don't press down. When the work is dry, unpin and smooth the sequins and beads into order.

Lining Fold over ⅝in/1.5cm of top and bottom lining and press. With RS tog, fold it in half to match bag shape and backstitch or machine straight stitch the sides together. Press the seams open.

Knitted bag With RS tog, backstitch the bottom and two sides together, using yarn double. Turn bag RS out. Sew frill sides up, RS tog, using yarn single.

With WS facing each other, insert lining into bag. Match up side seams. Slip stitch the lining to the knitted bag, all round the top edge, below the eyelet row.

Thread ribbon through eyelets.

chevron wrap

I love this combination of colors. The lemony pistachio-green of the *Kidsilk Aura* is so 1950s chic and, when teamed up with the mallard blue *Kidsilk Haze*, I think it is irresistible. When I was designing it, I started with the colors and then decided I wanted an easy, open-worked design. As well as the tantalizing color combination, the two yarns with their different ply lend textural interest to the stitch design. This is a simple chevron-striped wave or scallop pattern. Knitted on big needles, it positively zips along. And, thanks to the open nature of this design when knitted on bigger needles, it will hold its warmth around your shoulders or on your lap while remaining as light as a feather.

The lace—such as it is—is simple: just working yarn-forward and passing over of slipped stitches. I loved knitting it because, with only a six-row repeat, you gain ground really fast.

SKILL LEVEL
Easy

SIZE OF WRAP
The finished wrap measures 47¼in/120cm long by 25¼in/64cm wide.

YOU WILL NEED
Yarn A 4 x ⁷/₈oz/25g balls of Rowan *Kidsilk Aura* in light green (Pistachio, 766)
Yarn B 2 x ⁷/₈oz/25g balls of Rowan *Kidsilk Haze* in mallard blue (Trance, 582)
Pair of size 10 (6mm) needles

GAUGE
16.5 sts and 19 rows knitted to 4in/10cm square measured over pattern using both yarns as indicated and size 10 (6mm) needles *or needle size necessary to obtain correct gauge*.

ABBREVIATIONS
See page 116.

PATTERN NOTE
Yarn is held SINGLE throughout.

ALISON'S TIPS
• Carry the yarns not in use loosely up the side—there will be fewer ends to sew in and the yarns don't show that much on the side.
• The stitch number varies throughout and only goes back to what you started with on Rows 5 and 6, so don't count them before then or, if you do, don't panic!
• Cast on and bind off quite loosely.
• As it has quite a lot of stitches, you can knit this using a longish circular needle as if it was a pair of straight needles, if you prefer.

TO MAKE WRAP
Using size 10 (6mm) needles and yarn A, cast on 106 sts using thumb method (see page 12), loosely.
Row 1 (RS) K1, *skpo, K9, K2tog, rep from * to last st, K1.
Row 2 Purl.
Row 3 K1, *skpo, K7, K2tog, rep from * to last st, K1.
Row 4 Purl.
Row 5 K1, *skpo, yfwd [K1, yfwd] 5 times, K2tog, rep from * to last st, K1.
Row 6 Knit.
These 6 rows form chevron lace pattern.
Change to yarn B.
Repeat Rows 1 to 6.
Change to yarn A.
Repeat Rows 1 to 6.
Continue in this pattern/yarn sequence until work measures approx. 47¼in/120cm, ending with a yarn A sequence and after Row 5.
Bind off purlwise with WS facing.

TO FINISH
Sew in ends. Refer to ball bands for instructions. With WS facing up, pin out and press very lightly, using a damp pressing cloth and cool iron, taking care not to overpress the garter st ridges. Let dry fully before unpinning.

useful information

PRESSING AND AFTERCARE OF YOUR MOHAIR-MIX KNITTING

After knitting, some items will need to be pressed. Take care not to overdo this, as over-pressing can remove some of the lovely, hazy mohair fluff. If you need to press, pin the knitting out to size and shape, with the wrong side up, on a thick towel on your board or work surface. Using a very slightly damp cloth and a cool iron, hover and skim the iron over the work, don't rest it on the cloth or press down. Remove the cloth and leave the work in place until it is dry.

Some elements of the designs in this book do not require pressing, such as frills.

Because of their mohair content, and the delicate nature of mohair yarns, Rowan *Kidsilk Haze* and Rowan *Kidsilk Aura* must be hand-washed. Most other mohair-mix yarns require the same treatment, so be sure to refer to the yarn label for yarn care instructions. Mohair simply longs to become felt and the merest whisper of hot water will cause it to do so. Do not rub or wring the items as this will also encourage felting or, at best, matting. Always follow the instructions on the yarn label. It is best to use cool water and a light wool wash liquid. There are some no-rinse solutions, or alternatively, rinse twice in cool water. I never use fabric conditioner on mohair.

After washing, gently squeeze out the excess water to get the weight off the knitting. If it's a big item, I lie it sandwiched between two thick bath towels and give it a little massage to soak out more water.

Dry your knitting flat once you have re-shaped it.

KNITTING ABBREVIATIONS

The following are the abbreviations used in this book.

alt	alternate
approx.	approximately
beg	begin(ning)
cm	centimeter(s)
cont	continu(e)(ing)
dec	decreas(e)(ing)
foll	follow(s)(ing)
g	gram(s)
garter st	garter stitch (knit every row)
in	inch(es)
inc	increas(e)(ing)
K	knit
LH	left hand
m	meter(s)
M1	make one stitch by picking up horizontal strand between stitch just knit and next stitch and working into back of this loop (one stitch increased)
mm	millimeter(s)
oz	ounce(s)
P	purl
patt	pattern; or work in pattern
psso	pass slipped stitch over
rem	remain(s)(ing)
rep	repeat(ing)
rev st st	reverse stockinette stitch (purl all RS rows and knit all WS rows)
RH	right hand
RS	right side
skpo	slip 1 knitwise, knit 1, pass slipped stitch over (one stitch decreased)

sk2po	slip 1 stitch, knit 2 stitches together, pass the slipped stitch over the stitch made by knitting 2 together
sl	slip
st(s)	stitch(es)
st st	stockinette stitch (knit all RS rows and purl all WS rows)
tbl	through back of loop(s)
tog	together
WS	wrong side
wyib	take yarn to back of work
wyif	take yarn to front of work
yfrn	after knitting a stitch, bring yarn forward and take over RH needle and forward again before purling next stitch
yfwd	yarn forward (yarn forward between two needles and over RH needle to make a new stitch)
yo	yarn over needle (yarn over RH needle to make a new stitch)
yrn	yarn round needle (yarn over RH needle and to front again between two needles to make a new stitch)

[ ] *   Repeat instructions between square brackets, or after or between asterisks, as many times as instructed.

CROCHET ABBREVIATIONS

The simple crochet instructions in this book have been written using US crochet terminology. The UK equivalents for the UK crochet terminology used in this book are as follows:

US	UK
chain (ch)	chain (ch)
single crochet (sc)	double crochet (dc)
skip (a stitch)	miss (a stitch)

YARN INFORMATION

The following are the specifications of the Rowan yarns used for the designs in this book (see page 118 for the yarn-weight symbols). It is always best to try to obtain the exact yarns specified in the patterns, but when substituting yarn, remember to calculate the yarn amount needed by yardage/meterage rather than by ball weight. For yarn care directions, refer to the yarn label.

Rowan *Cotton Glacé*

A lightweight pure cotton yarn; 100 percent fine cotton; 1¾oz/50g (approx. 126yd/115m) per ball; 23 sts and 32 rows to 4in/10cm measured over st st using sizes 3–5 (3.25–3.75mm) knitting needles.

Rowan *Fine Milk Cotton*

A super-fine-weight cotton mix yarn; 70 percent cotton; 30 percent milk protein; 1¾oz/50g (approx. 164yd/150m) per ball; 30 sts and 38 rows to 4in/10cm measured over st st using size 2 (2.25mm) knitting needles.

Rowan *Kid Classic*

An Aran-weight mohair-lambswool yarn; 70 percent lambswool; 26 percent kid mohair; 4 percent nylon; 1¾oz/50g (approx. 153yd/140m) per ball; 18–19sts and 23–25 rows to 4in/10cm measured over st st using sizes 8–9 (5–5.5mm) knitting needles.

Rowan *Kidsilk Aura*

A medium-weight mohair-mix yarn; 75 percent kid mohair, 25 percent silk; ⁷⁄₈oz/25g (approx. 82yd/75m) per ball; 16–20 sts and 19–28 rows to 4in/10cm measured over st st using sizes 6–10 (4–6mm) knitting needles.

Rowan *Kidsilk Haze*

A lightweight mohair-mix yarn; 70 percent super kid mohair, 30 percent silk; ⁷⁄₈oz/25g (approx. 229yd/210m) per ball; 18–25 sts and 23–34 rows to 4in/10cm measured over st st using sizes 3–8 (3.25–5mm) knitting needles.

(continued on next page)

Rowan *Pure Wool 4 ply*

A super-fine pure wool yarn; 100 percent superwash wool; 1¾oz/50g (approx. 174yd/160m) per ball; 28 sts and 36 rows to 4in/10cm measured over st st using sizes 3–8 (3.25–5mm) knitting needles.

Rowan *Shimmer*

A super-fine-weight yarn; 60 percent cupro; 40 percent polyester; ⅞oz/25g (approx. 191yd/175m) per ball; 29–34 sts and 36–40 rows to 4in/10cm measured over st st using sizes 2–3 (2.25–3.25mm) knitting needles.

STANDARD YARN-WEIGHT SYSTEM

Categories of yarn, gauge ranges, and recommended knitting needle sizes from the Craft Yarn Council of America.
YarnStandards.com

Yarn-weight symbol and category names	0 LACE	1 SUPER FINE	2 FINE	3 LIGHT	4 MEDIUM	5 BULKY	6 SUPER BULKY
Types of yarns** in category	no. 10 crochet cotton, fingering	sock, fingering, baby, 4-ply	sport, baby	light worsted, DK	worsted, afghan, Aran	chunky, craft, rug	bulky, roving
Knit gauge ranges* in st st to 4in/10cm	33–40*** sts	27–32 sts	23–26 sts	21–24 sts	16–20 sts	12–15 sts	6–11 sts
Recommended needle in metric size range	1.5–2.25 mm	2.25–3.25 mm	3.25–3.75 mm	3.75–4.5 mm	4.5–5.5 mm	6.5–8 mm	8mm and larger
Recommended needle in US size range	000 to 1	1 to 3	3 to 5	5 to 7	7 to 9	9 to 11	11 and larger

* GUIDELINES ONLY The above reflect the most commonly used gauges and needle sizes for specific yarn categories.

** The generic yarn-weight names in the yarn categories include those commonly used in the UK and US.

*** Ultra-fine lace-weight yarns are difficult to put into gauge ranges; always follow the gauge given in your pattern for these yarns.

ROWAN YARN SUPPLIERS

Rowan yarns are widely distributed. To find a yarn store near you, contact Westminster Fibers Inc. (see below) or visit the Rowan website for a list of online suppliers:

www.knitrowan.com

USA

Westminster Fibers Inc.,
165 Ledge Street, Nashua,
NH 03060.
Tel: 1-800-445-9276.
E-mail: rowan@westminsterfibers.com
www.westminsterfibers.com

AUSTRALIA

Australian Country Spinners,
314 Albert Street, Brunswick,
Victoria 3056.
Tel: (61) 3 9380 3888.
Fax: (61) 3 9387 2674.
E-mail: sales@auspinners.com.au

AUSTRIA

Coats Harlander GmbH,
Autokaderstrasse 31, A-1210 Wien.
Tel: (01) 27716-0.
Fax: (01) 27716-228.

BELGIUM

Coats Benelux, Ring Oost 14A,
Ninove, 9400.
Tel: 0346 35 37 00.
E-mail: sales.coatsninove@coats.com

CANADA

Same as USA.

CHINA

Coats Shanghai Ltd.,
No. 9 Building, Boasheng Road,
Songjiang Industrial Zone,
Shanghai, 201613.
Tel: (86-21) 5774 3733.
Fax: (86-21) 5774 3768.

DENMARK

Coats Danmark A/S, Nannagade 28,
2200 Kobenhavn N.
Tel: 35 86 90 50.
Fax: 35 82 15 10.
E-mail: info@hpgruppen.dk
www.hpgruppen.dk

FINLAND

Coats Opti Oy, Ketjutie 3,
04220 Kerava.
Tel: (358) 9 274 871.
Fax: (358) 9 2748 7330.
E-mail: coatsopti.sales@coats.com

FRANCE

Coats France/Steiner Fréres,
SAS 100 avenue du Général de Gaulle,
18 500 Mehun-Sur-Yèvre.
Tel: 02 48 23 12 30.
Fax: 02 48 23 12 40.

GERMANY

Coats GMbH, Kaiserstrasse 1,
D-79341 Kenzingen.
Tel: 7644 8020.
Fax: 7644 802399.
www.coatsgmbh.de

HOLLAND

Same as Belgium.

HONG KONG

Coats China Holding Ltd.,
19/F Millennium City 2, 378 Kwun
Tong Road, Kwun Tong, Kowloon.
Tel: (852) 2798 6886.
Fax: (852) 2305 0311.

ICELAND

Storkurinn, Laugavegi 59,
101 Reykjavik.
Tel: (354) 551 8258.
E-mail: storkurinn@simnet.is

ITALY

Coats Cucirini srl, Via Sarca 223,
20126 Milano.
Tel: 800 992377.
Fax: 0266111701.
E-mail: servizio.clienti@coats.com

JAPAN

Puppy-Jardin Co. Ltd.,
3-8 11 Kudanminami, Chiyodaku,
Hiei Kudan Bldg. 5F, Tokyo.
Tel: (81) 3 3222-7076.
Fax: (81) 3 3222-7066.
E-mail: info@rowan-jaeger.com

KOREA

Coats Korea Co. Ltd., 5F Kuckdong
B/D, 935-40 Bangbae-Dong,
Seocho-Gu, Seoul.
Tel: (82) 2 521 6262.
Fax: (82) 2 521 5181

LEBANON

y.knot, Saifi Village,
Mkhalissiya Street 162, Beirut.
Tel: (961) 1 992211.
Fax: (961) 1 315553.
E-mail: yknot@cyberia.net.lb

(continued on next page)

LUXEMBERG
Same as Belgium.

MEXICO
Estambres Crochet SA de CV,
Aaron Saenz 1891-7,
Monterrey, NL 64650.
Tel: +52 (81) 8335-3870.

NEW ZEALAND
ACS New Zealand, 1 March Place,
Belfast, Christchurch.
Tel: 64-3-323-6665.
Fax: 64-3-323-6660.

NORWAY
Coats Knappehuset AS,
Pb 100 Ulset,
5873 Bergen.
Tel: (47) 55 53 93 00.
Fax: (47) 55 53 93 93.

SINGAPORE
Golden Dragon Store,
101 Upper Cross Street #02-51,
People's Park Centre, Singapore
058357. Tel: (65) 6 5358454.
Fax: (65) 6 2216278.
E-mail: gdscraft@hotmail.com

SOUTH AFRICA
Arthur Bales PTY, P.O. BOX 44644,
62 4th Avenue, Linden 2104.
Tel: (27) 11 888 2401.
Fax: (27) 11 782 6137.

SPAIN
Oyambre, Pau Claris 145,
80009 Barcelona.
Tel: (34) 670 011957.
Fax: (34) 93 4872672.
E-mail: oyambre@oyambreonline.com

Coats Fabra, Sant Adria 20,
08030 Barcelona.
Tel: 93 2908400. Fax: 93 2908409.
E-mail: atencion.clientes@coats.com

SWEDEN
Coats Expotex AB, Division Craft,
Box 297, 401 24 Göteborg.
Tel: (46) 33 720 79 00.
Fax: (46) 31 47 16 50.

SWITZERLAND
Coats Stroppel AG, Stroppelstrasse 16,
CH-5300 Tungi (AG).
Tel: 056 298 12 20.
Fax: 056 298 12 50.

TAIWAN
Cactus Quality Co. Ltd., P.O. Box 30 485,
Taipei.
Office: 7Fl-2, No. 140, Roosevelt Road,
Sec 2, Taipei.
Tel: 886-2-23656527.
Fax: 886-2-23656503.
E-mail: cqcl@m17.hinet.net

THAILAND
Global Wide Trading,
10 Lad Prao Soi 88, Bangkok 10310.
Tel: 00 662 933 9019.
Fax: 00 662 933 9110.
E-mail: theneedleworld@yahoo.com

UK
Rowan, Green Lane Mill,
Holmfirth,
West Yorkshire HD9 2DX.
Tel: +44 (0) 1484 681881.
Fax: +44 (0) 1484 687920.
E-mail: mail@knitrowan.com

Author's acknowledgments

My grateful thanks to the following: Mark, Florence, and Lily who have patiently endured another year of mohair, but this time possibly with extra cussin' due to the lace; to Susan Berry, with whom I love working; to John Heseltine for yet more gorgeous pictures and Anne Wilson for laying them out to such great effect; to Rowan for the stunning yarn and your continuing support; to Penny Hill, pattern writer; and Donna Jones, pattern checker to the confused (and super friend); and Katie Hardwicke for editorial help; to Nathalie Heseltine, Juliette Manning, and Holly Walker for modeling; to Light Locations for some of the locations; to Emma, Kay, and Alison at Lana Pura and all my other knitting and non-knitting friends who have been so encouraging and supportive; and to my lovely knitting workshop customers: you are my "guinea pigs" (did you know that? I do hope you don't mind!), and often, you are my inspiration, too.